At Issue

| Date Rape

Other Books in the At Issue series:

At Issue

| Date Rape

Christine Watkins, Book Editor

GREENHAVEN PRESS

An imprint of Thomson Gale, a part of The Thomson Corporation

Detroit • New York • San Francisco • New Haven, Conn. • Waterville, Maine • London

HV
6561
D35
2007

Christine Nasso, *Publisher*
Elizabeth Des Chenes, *Managing Editor*

© 2007 The Gale Group.

Star logo is a trademark and Gale and Greenhaven Press are registered trademarks used herein under license.

For more information, contact:
Greenhaven Press
27500 Drake Rd.
Farmington Hills, MI 48331-3535
Or you can visit our Internet site at http://www.gale.com

LIBRARY OF CONGRESS CATALOGING-IN-PUBLICATION DATA

Date Rape / Christine Watkins, book editor.
   p. cm. -- (At issue)
   Includes bibliographical references and index.
   ISBN-13: 978-0-7377-3681-6 (hardcover)
   ISBN-13: 978-0-7377-3682-3 (pbk.)
   1. Date rape--United States. I. I. Watkins, Christine 1951-
   HV6561.D35 2007
   362.883--dc22

                 2007019463

ISBN-10: 0-7377-3681-X (hardcover)
ISBN-10: 0-7377-3682-8 (pbk.)

Printed in the United States of America
10 9 8 7 6 5 4 3 2 1

Contents

Introduction

Date rape is a serious crime, one that can leave the victim with lifelong feelings of anxiety, depression, self-blame, and betrayal. But date rape is also one of the most difficult crimes to prove. Simply put, date rape—or any rape, for that matter—is sex without the *consent* of both parties. However, exactly what constitutes consent has not been established. Thus, the problem with proving a rape occurred and, more importantly, preventing a rape from occurring in the first place lies with the fact that males and females interpret behavioral signals, including consent, differently.

Take, for example, the date rape case involving Kobe Bryant, the professional basketball player with the Los Angeles Lakers. On the night of June 30, 2003, in a Colorado hotel, Kobe Bryant met Katelyn Faber, a desk clerk. They talked and flirted with each other, and eventually Bryant asked her to go to his room, which she willingly did. The next morning Faber went to the police and accused Bryant of rape. According to the sheriff's deputies who interviewed her, Faber did not initially resist when Bryant hugged and kissed her. But when she did ask him to stop, he blocked her from leaving, gripped her around the neck, forced her over a chair, and raped her. Bryant admitted to the police that he had sex with her that night, but claimed it was consensual. The case was dismissed before going to trial because Katelyn Faber did not want to testify or participate. After the dismissal, Kobe Bryant gave a statement for the public: "Although I truly believe this encounter between us was consensual, I recognize now that she did not and does not view this incident the same way I did. . . . I now understand how she feels that she did not consent to this encounter."

To further complicate the issue of consent, in January 2003, the California Supreme Court ruled that even if a woman initially consents to sex, she can change her mind at any time during the sexual act, after which her partner must stop immediately or be charged with rape. The case in point involved two seventeen-year-olds. During sexual intercourse the girl told the boy, "I have to go home." He then asked her to "give me some time," and did not stop until a minute or two later. He was convicted of rape. In her ruling, Justice Ming W. Chin wrote, "Forcible rape occurs when, during apparently consensual intercourse, the victim expresses an objection and attempts to stop the act and the defendant forcibly continues despite the objection." Instead of establishing explicit and reasonable standards by which to determine consent, many lawyers and researchers believe that this ruling creates even more troubling questions. For instance, without clearly saying the word "no" or "stop," how is the withdrawal of consent to be communicated? And how much time is allowed for someone to stop after consent has been rescinded? In her dissenting vote in the case, Justice Janice Rogers Brown noted that the ruling "does not tell us how soon would have been soon enough. Ten seconds? Thirty? A minute?" She also addressed another crucial point: "Is persistence the same thing as force? And even if we conclude persistence should be criminalized in this situation, should the penalty be the same as for forcible rape?"

If the defining characteristics of force and consent are confusing enough on their own, the addition of alcohol distorts them even more. A 2004 study by the Harvard School of Public Health found that alcohol use is a central factor in most college rapes, and that nearly 75 percent of college rapes reported in a seven-month period happened when the victim was intoxicated. This could be in large part because the victim may have been too drunk to refuse, and if she did refuse, the perpetrator may have been too drunk to comprehend her refusal. Feminists, or those who demand equality of the sexes, will argue that women should have the right to drink alcohol

without fear of being raped, and that men n⁄
treat women with respect. Others will argue tn.
should take responsibility for their actions and not put ⌐
selves in harm's way in the first place. Mary P. Koss, PhD, professor of public health at the University of Arizona and co-
author of the study "Correlates of Rape while Intoxicated in a
National Sample of College Women," believes both parties
should be held accountable. "Men need education about what
constitutes rape, and women should be better informed of
strategies to avoid risky situations."

The persistent rewriting and reforming of rape laws,
though done with righteous intentions, continue to leave questions unresolved—questions about consent, force, and culpa-
bility. These and other issues are further discussed by the authors in *At Issue: Date Rape*.

1

Drugs Are the Culprit in Many Date Rapes

Cynthia M. Piccolo

Cynthia M. Piccolo has written numerous articles about health-related issues for MedHunters.com.

Since the late 1990s drug-induced sexual assaults have increased throughout the United States, Canada, and abroad, and are concentrated among high school, college, and university students. However, it is difficult to establish exact statistics because date rape drugs impair memory and leave the system quickly. The three most common date rape drugs are Rohypnol, gamma hydroxybutyrate (GHB), and Ketamine; they are extremely dangerous because they can incapacitate victims and cause respiratory arrest. To minimize the risk of being drugged, all drinks—including nonalcoholic beverages—should be carefully monitored.

In the late 1980s, I had a summer job at a sexual assault crisis center. One of my duties was to enter files of sexual assault victims into a database. While I remember some women saying they were drunk at the time their assault occurred (and indeed, alcohol continues to be a date rape "drug," with some statistics saying that 50% of women raped by acquaintances reported being drunk at the time), none reported having been drugged. But since the late 1990s, things have changed:

> "Four men were sentenced to prison Thursday [April 6, 2000] after being convicted in one of the nation's first trials involving a death linked to a date-rape drug. The three men

who were convicted of manslaughter were sentenced to up to 15 years in prison; a fourth man convicted of being an accessory to manslaughter after the fact was sentenced to up to five years. . . . Prosecutors alleged the men gave [Fifteen-year-old victim] Samantha a soft drink secretly spiked with GHB [gamma hydroxybutyrate] during a Jan. 16, 1999, party. . . . She died the next day. Her friend Melanie Sindone, now 16, also ingested the drug [and] was briefly in a coma, but survived." (CBSNews.com, April 12, 2000)

"*Harvard Crimson* said two Harvard students had been treated for Rohypnol poisoning after attending off-campus parties. Rohypnol is frequently used as a date-rape drug because it induces unconsciousness within minutes. . . . Some estimates place cases of Rohypnol-induced sexual assault in the United States at 5,000 this year alone." (MIT News Office, November 5, 2003)

"A Vancouver man faces a criminal charge after his three-year-old girl drank from a water bottle spiked with a so-called date-rape drug. The toddler was playing in her home on Vancouver's west side on Sunday when she suddenly appeared to be having a seizure. After calling emergency services, the girl's father realized that she had taken a drink from a water bottle containing GHB, best known as a date-rape drug." (CBC.ca, December 14, 2004)

"Traces of a 'date rape' drug were found in blood samples from two of the nine women who were hospitalized after attending University of Colorado fraternity parties last month, police said Thursday. One of the doses was potentially fatal." (TheDenverChannel.com, October 6, 2005)

"Two weeks ago, emergency room doctors told Alexandra, 19, she likely ended up in the intensive care unit because an amaretto and Coke she was drinking at a party the night before was spiked with what is often called a 'date rape drug.'" (*The Journal* (Queen's University), December 1, 2005)

Stories similar to the above excerpts are seen regularly in the media in communities in the United States, Canada, and abroad. Of course, despite the use of the term "date rape drug," rape is not always the (only) result of ingesting the substance—it may be hospitalization or death.

Since these drugs can be slipped into soft drinks as well as alcoholic beverages, being a teetotaler won't necessarily save you.

In the United States, as cited above, some estimates place cases of Rohypnol-induced sexual assault alone at 5,000 for the year 2003. However, numbers are difficult to establish for many reasons, including: a lack of reporting mechanisms; because these drugs impair memory; because the drugs may no longer be in a victim's system once an assault is reported; and because sexual assaults are generally underreported (it is estimated that two to six times more rapes occur than are actually reported). In Canada, according to a study published in the November/December 2004 issue of the *Canadian Journal of Public Health*, not only have drug-facilitated sexual assaults increased in the past decade, but more than one in four hospital-reported sexual assaults were drug-facilitated. Overall, in both the United States and Canada, incidents are concentrated among high school, college, and university students.

The Usual Suspects

The two main date rape drugs are Rohypnol and GHB, but ketamine is also sometimes used.

- **Rohypnol**, or flunitrazepam (also known as roofies, forget-me pill, Mexican valium, mind erasers, etc.)— This is a benzodiazepine (central nervous system depressant) like Valium, but 10 times more potent. Rohypnol is a tasteless and odorless drug that comes in pill form and can be dissolved in liquid. It is widely available in Europe, Mexico, and Colombia, but is neither manufactured nor approved for sale in the United

States or in Canada. Illicit use of Rohypnol began in the 1970s in Europe and appeared in the United States in the early 1990s. Much of the concern surrounding Rohypnol is its abuse as a date rape drug, for as the National Institute on Drug Abuse (NIDA) explains: "Rohypnol can incapacitate victims and prevent them from resisting sexual assault. It can produce 'antero-grade amnesia,' which means individuals may not remember events they experienced while under the effects of the drug. Also, Rohypnol may be lethal when mixed with alcohol and/or other depressants."

- **GHB**, or gamma hydroxybutyrate (also known as liquid ecstasy, liquid X, soap, Grievous Bodily Harm, easy lay, etc.)—This is a central nervous system depressant, and according to NIDA, it was widely available in the US in health food stores during the 1980s, but non-prescription sales were banned in 1990. The drug takes effect within about 15 minutes of ingestion and, depending on dose, can last several hours. Aside from decreasing inhibitions and causing drowsiness, it can cause nausea, numbness, convulsions, and respiratory arrest. This drug comes as a liquid, pill, or powder, and has a salty or soapy taste, but fruity or flavored drinks or alcohol can mask the taste.

- **Ketamine**, or ketamine hydrochloride (also known as special K, K, kit-kat, etc.)—This drug was derived from phencyclidine (PCP) in the 1960s for use as a dissocia-tive anesthetic, and causes anesthesia without respira-tory depression. It is a white powder, and is often used as an animal tranquilizer. The effects of this drug ap-pear rapidly, and include a dissociative state leading to floating/out-of-body experiences and hallucinations. According to an article by Dr. Paul M. Gahlinger, on the American Academy of Family Physicians website, other common effects include: ". . . confusion, antero-grade amnesia, and delirium. They also may experience tachycardia, palpitations, hypertension, and respiratory depression with apnea. 'Flashbacks' or visual distur-bances can be experienced days or weeks after inges-tion."

Other substances implicated in unwanted sexual activity, in addition to alcohol itself, are marijuana, benzodiazepines, cocaine, heroin, and amphetamines.

Minimizing the Risk

Since these drugs can be slipped into soft drinks as well as al-coholic beverages, being a teetotaler won't necessarily save you. In order to minimize risk:

- Don't accept drinks from strangers.

- Don't accept drinks you haven't opened yourself.

- Don't accept drinks coming from large, open contain-ers, such as punch bowls.

- Drink bottled or canned drinks, and when you hold the drink, hold it with your thumb over the opening.

- If you are drinking something out of a glass, hold it from the top, with your hand arched over the mouth of the glass.

- Don't leave drinks unattended.

- If you think your drink may have been tampered with, don't drink it—pour it out.

- Keep an eye on yourself and friends for any changes in behavior, particularly if you or they appear to be much more intoxicated than expected, given the alcohol con-sumed. It's a good idea to have your designated driver doing double duty watching out for everyone.

- If you think you've been drugged, go to the hospital with a friend, family member, or the police. (And if you can, keep the beverage for analysis.)

2

Alcohol Contributes to Most Cases of Date Rape

Roger Dobson and Sarah Kate Templeton

Roger Dobson and Sarah Kate Templeton are writers for the Sunday Times *(London).*

It is widely perceived that women who do not keep a watchful eye on their drinks are susceptible to date rape drugs, and in turn, sexual assault. However, a report published in the Journal of Clinical Forensic Medicine *found that a combination of alcohol and recreational drugs such as marijuana and cocaine makes women vulnerable to attack more often than do date rape drugs. In fact, researchers found a link between sexual assault and date rape drugs in only 2 percent of reported cases. People need to be alert against spiked drinks, but even more alert against drinking heavily.*

A STUDY has found that women are mistakenly blaming spiked drinks for making them vulnerable to sexual assaults.

The analysis of more than 1,000 cases by the Forensic Science Service (FSS) has shown that by drinking heavily and taking recreational drugs, women are actually making themselves vulnerable to sex attacks.

The finding is at odds with the widespread perception that women who fail to stay alert in bars can fall prey to men who spike their drinks.

Roger Dobson and Sarah Kate Templeton, "Drink the Real Culprit in Date-rape Drug Claims," *The Sunday Times—Britain*, July 31, 2005. Reproduced by permission.

Researchers established that in only 2% of cases was there a direct link between a sexual assault and drinks spiked with so-called date-rape drugs.

The FSS, an agency reporting to the Home Office, investigated 1,014 samples from women who complained that their drinks had been spiked.

Heavy drinking meant women were often not in a fit state to give proper consent to sex.

In only 21 cases were traces of drugs found where the complainant had not taken them voluntarily. Rohypnol, perceived as the most common date-rape drug, was not found in a single sample.

Recreational Drugs—Not Date Rape Drugs

The report, published in the *Journal of Clinical Forensic Medicine*, suggests that a combination of drink and recreational drugs such as cannabis, cocaine and amphetamines could be causing women to become drowsy or lose their inhibitions.

Sixty-five per cent of the tested samples contained either alcohol, illegal drugs or both. Alcohol was detected in 46% of cases and recreational drugs in 34%. The findings prompted the report's authors, Michael Scott-Ham and Fiona Burton of the FSS, to warn: "Advice should be given on sensible drinking and risks of recreational drugs use."

The message that women themselves may be responsible could be hard to accept. So entrenched is the belief in date-rape drugs that in 2003 a short film highlighting the dangers was launched in cinemas.

The film, *Spiked!*, funded by the charity DrugScope, showed a man chatting up a girl before spiking her drink. The final shot depicted the girl alone and dishevelled. A postscript asked: "Who's watching your drink?" In a few samples in the new study drugs were found that the woman had not admitted taking, including ecstasy, GHB (gamma hydroxybutyrate), diazepam and temazepam.

GHB disappears from the bloodstream after eight hours and can be detected in urine samples for only 18 hours.

We believe alcohol is the big problem. There are assailants who will prey on people who are incapacitated through alcohol use.

The authors acknowledged that because only about 35% of the samples were taken during this period, there could have been additional spiking with GHB that they did not detect. However, in the samples they did take in the required period, GHB was found in only two cases, suggesting it was not commonly used as a date-rape drug. Some of the victims had been sedated by a combination of alcohol and the prescription medicines they were taking.

Health experts warned heavy drinking meant women were often not in a fit state to give proper consent to sex.

Dr Cath White, clinical director of the St Mary's sexual assault referral centre in Manchester, said: "Drug-assisted sexual assault is happening but just not on the scale that has been suggested.

"We have been saying all along that we believe alcohol is the big problem. There are assailants who will prey on people who are incapacitated through alcohol use."

Insistence on Date Rape Drugs

Some victims are not convinced by the findings. Kim Shannon, who lives in Glasgow, was raped by two men five years ago when she was 16.

"I passed out so quickly the drink must have been spiked, but the toxicologist's report could not find any trace of a drug," she said. "But it was 9am the next morning when I was tested and it was 6pm the previous evening that I had had the drink.

"The report didn't say I hadn't been drugged, but that no trace of the drug had been found."

Shannon cannot remember what happened from 6pm until 2am, but the police doctor found carpet burns on her back, a cut above her eye and bite and nail marks on her body.

Bahar Ali, 36, and Stephen Singh, 22, were convicted of causing clandestine injury having sex with an unconscious woman. Ali was jailed for five years and Singh for four.

"At first the police were reluctant to prosecute," said Shannon. "It was my word against theirs and I couldn't remember a thing. I don't think that could just have been the alcohol."

Test Results Point to Alcohol

A team led by Ian Hindmarch, professor of human psychopharmacology at Surrey University, has analysed 3,000 urine samples from Americans who claimed to have been victims of date rape. He said the commonest drug found was alcohol.

"Detailed testing does not support the contention that any single drug apart from alcohol can be particularly identified as a date-rape drug," he said. "I do not say drug-assisted sexual assault doesn't happen but it was alcohol that was making victims liable to be abused."

3

Alcohol Is Not the Cause of Date Rape

Scott Hampton

Scott Hampton is director of Ending the Violence and the Consexuality Project, a sexual violence prevention initiative.

Although drinking alcohol and sexual assault often happen together, alcohol does not cause the violence. Yes, drinking alcohol reduces inhibitions, making it easier to violate sexual boundaries; and if the victim is intoxicated, she is less able to protect herself against an attack. But the underlying cause is not alcohol abuse—it is sexual violence. And those who perpetrate sexual assault should be held accountable and not allowed to minimize their violence by blaming the effects of alcohol.

Alcohol and sexual assault often happen together. According to some research, 30 percent of all sexual assaults occur when the perpetrator is under the influence of alcohol. In some cases, the victim is also intoxicated. Drinking makes it easy for the perpetrator to ignore sexual boundaries, while the victim's intoxication makes it more difficult for her to guard against an attack.

A common misunderstanding is that if people commit sexual assaults only when drunk, then (a) the drinking must have caused the assault and (b) sobriety and alcohol counseling are adequate to prevent future assaults. These erroneous conclusions confuse correlation and causation. To illustrate, consider the correlation between consciousness and sexual as-

Scott Hampton, "Alcohol and Sexual Assault: The Connection," *Alcohol Problems & Solutions*, January 23, 2005. Reproduced by permission.

sault. Perpetrators of sexual assault typically commit sexual assaults only when they are awake, but it would be ridiculous to suggest that being awake caused them to commit sexual assaults. So, what is the relationship between alcohol and sexual violence?

The Relationship Between Alcohol and Sexual Assault

First, alcohol use does not cause sexual violence. Putting alcohol into your system does not cause you to commit a sexual assault anymore than putting gasoline into your car causes you to drive to the airport. Gasoline makes it easier to do what you want to do (e.g., drive a car) while alcohol also makes it easier to do what you want to do (e.g., grope women). If you do not at least think about doing something when sober, you are not likely to do it when drunk. For example, no one worries about becoming so intoxicated that he will lose control and stab himself in the eye with a fork. Why? Because he would never consider doing that when sober.

Alcohol acts as a permission slip. By reducing inhibitions, alcohol often makes it more likely that someone will choose to sexually assault another person. As one man in a violent offender program noted, "When I first came to your program I told you that I hit my wife because I was drunk; now I realize that I drank so that I could hit her." He realized that alcohol did not excuse or even explain the abuse. Instead, alcohol was the way that he had tried to avoid responsibility for the abuse.

Alcohol Should Not Be an Excuse

Sexual assault occurs despite alcohol use, not because of it. When someone is extremely intoxicated, we call that person "impaired." "Impaired" means that you have more difficulty performing tasks. Therefore, if you are going to sexually assault someone when drunk, you have to try harder, focus your attention and be more determined than if you were sober. In effect, people who sexually assault when drunk, do so, not because they are intoxicated, but despite their intoxication. They have to overcome the impairment to commit the sexual assault.

Memory loss is not the same as lack of intent. If a perpetrator of sexual assault claims that he has no specific recollection of the assault, that does not mean that he had no intention of doing it at the time. All it means is that the perpetrator is currently either unable or unwilling to report his state of mind when the assaults occurred. For example, sometimes we hear perpetrators report on events that were acceptable (e.g., "I remember drinking and dancing") but not the events that could result in arrest and prosecution (e.g., "I don't recall fondling that person"). Or the perpetrator will not recall the offense, but will be able to assert with confidence what his state of mind was at the time (e.g., "I had no desire for sexual gratification"). How can you NOT remember what you did, but be absolutely certain what your motives were when you did it? How does alcohol know which memories to delete and which to keep intact?

Sexual assault and substance abuse are separate issues. If someone violates sexual boundaries while drunk, that person has two problems that need to be addressed. Taking responsibility for alcohol consumption addresses only half of the problem. The perpetrator also needs to take responsibility for the sexual violence. On the most basic level, the perpetrator needs to learn that all sexual contact without permission is sexual violence.

Sexual Consent Is Imperative

To address this, good sex offender programs teach the principles of sexual consent. These principles are:

1. Privilege. Sex is never a right; it is always a privilege, an honor, a gift that can either be granted or taken away by the person you wish to have contact with.

2. Permission. Since sexual contact is always a privilege, you always must seek permission before initiating contact. In addition, you need to be sober enough to know whether or not you have been given permission. Permission requires that the other person is capable, at the time, of giving you permission (e.g., that person is old enough, sober enough, and not coerced by you to say "Yes.") If the other person is afraid to say "No" because you have a position of power or authority, you cannot know whether your potential sexual partner truly wishes to have contact with you (even if he or she does not actively resist your advances).

3. Justification/Intent. There is no excuse for engaging in sexual contact without consent. Sexually respectful people adopt the philosophy of "First Do No Harm." Those who do not respect sexual boundaries should not be allowed to explain or minimize their use of aggression as the result of alcohol or drug use, stress, deviant arousal patterns, loss of control or misunderstandings.

4. Responsibility. The only person who ever is responsible for a sexual assault is the perpetrator. The victim never is. We, as members of their community, share responsibility for holding perpetrators accountable for their violence. How do we do this? By never blaming victims for the harm they suffered. By remembering that sexual violence is not "just a part of the disease of alcoholism." By never letting a perpetrator's sexual access and satisfaction become more important than the victim's sexual safety and autonomy. By keeping these principles in mind, we can make great strides in achieving sexual safety in our community.

4

Young Men Must Understand What Constitutes Rape

Mike Hardcastle

Mike Hardcastle is a volunteer youth worker, special-needs foster parent, and teen mentor.

Rape occurs every two minutes in North America, yet society still has no definitive concept of what it entails. Regardless of the confusion, young men need to be clear about date rape because it is a serious sex crime with consequences that can last a lifetime. The most important thing to keep in mind is that no means no. If at any time a partner indicates—verbally or physically—she (or he) does not want to go any further, the sexual contact must not go any further. And if either partner is intoxicated, sexual intercourse must not occur; reduced inhibitions do not negate responsibilities. Even during the thrill of the moment, young men must protect themselves by understanding the serious repercussions that can result from having sex.

Call it date rape, call it acquaintance rape, or just call it what it is, rape; whatever you call it, it's a crime and it is committed at a shocking rate of every 2 minutes in North America. While public education about rape has made great strides in the past decades, particularly in the area of victim blaming and shaming, many guys still just don't seem to get it when it comes to date rape. Sure we all know that forcing yourself on a girl is rape but when we picture this we usually imagine a violent attack, sometimes with a weapon, or drug-

Mike Hardcastle, "What Every Guy Must Know About Date Rape," teenadvice.about .com, April 12, 2006. Reproduced by permission.

ging a girl with a date rape drug, yet there are other ways to coerce or instigate an unwanted sexual encounter that some guys may not even think about. Often non-violent on the surface and sometimes the result of mixed messages, not listening, wishful thinking, and/or diminished capacity on the part of one or both parties, date rape is one of the most misunderstood and controversial of sex crimes.

In date rape scenarios many guys really don't feel that they have crossed a line or done anything wrong and this is the biggest part of the problem. Society still sends a very mixed message on this topic with many people feeling that date rape is most often the result of miscommunication or misunderstanding rather than a true act of criminal intent. Regardless of society's confusion the law remains clear and we want to lay it on the line for all you guys out there in a no-uncertain-terms kind of way. Guys, believe it or not it is in your best interest to really get it where date rape is concerned because a date rape conviction is still a sex crime conviction and can follow you for the rest of your life. Here it is, the bottom line on date rape.

"No" Means "Stop"

Date rape, also called acquaintance rape, is rape that occurs between two people who know one another and usually happens in social situations. It can happen between people who are dating as a couple and have had consensual sex in the past. It can happen between two people who are starting to date. It can happen between people who are just friends and it can happen between people who are friends of friends, a.k.a. acquaintances. You do not have to be on a date for a date rape to occur. The first and most important thing a guy needs to understand is that NO MEANS NO. This is a non-negotiable fact. As soon as the word "No," comes out of her mouth you must stop what you are doing and you should not persist by trying again. Even if it is a hot and heavy make out session as soon as she puts the brakes on you must stop. Even if the kissing starts up again you must not move things any further than she clearly indicates she wants them to go. If you have even a shadow of a doubt about what she really wants you must stop altogether. Believe it or not guys, this is for your protection as much as it is for hers. Try not to lose sight of this fact. By stopping when she asks or when it is clear she is uncomfortable you are not only thinking of her (which is important) but you are protecting yourself. For everybody's sake when she says "No," or starts physically pushing you away even without saying no, or if she repeatedly stops you from moving past a certain point (for example: she is OK with kissing but physically stops you when you try to reach under her clothes—even without saying "no") you MUST STOP. Just because she is OK with the kissing doesn't mean she wants more. Kissing you is not a promise of giving in to anything you may want. Think of it this way, when you willingly give a buddy a ride home one day does that automatically mean you'll do it everyday or that you'll also start driving them to work and on errands as well? No, of course not. Consenting to one thing does not mean you are consenting to the same thing in the future, nor does it mean that you are consenting to similar or related things. This is the case with sexual contact. Just because a girl consents to one type of sexual interaction does not automatically mean she is open to others. Just because a girl has had sex with you in the past does not mean that she is obligated to have sex with you every time you get intimate together.

If you are under the influence do not have sex.

Intoxication Is No Excuse

Another area of confusion on the date rape topic is intoxication. Bottom line, if a girl is intoxicated she cannot consent to sex and you could be charged with rape. It does not matter whether you knew she was intoxicated, it doesn't matter if you were intoxicated too, all that matters is that she was not in a state of mind to consent and therefore it is rape. If you get a girl drunk or high and then "get together" with her you have committed a sexual assault. Again, it doesn't matter if you are drunk or high as well. Your diminished abilities do not negate your responsibilities. A good rule to follow; if you are under the influence do not have sex. Now say you really had no idea a girl was intoxicated and that she truly appeared to be a willing partner, what then? The reality is that you could still be charged with rape if she is able to prove she was drunk or high. Your knowledge of her state may only be a mitigating factor; it does not guarantee you won't be charged. So another good rule to follow, don't have sex with anybody you are not 100% certain is able to consent. In other words, don't have sex with somebody you don't know very well or have not spent most of your time with immediately before your sexual encounter. While it may seem unfair to say to a guy "Dude, you're under the influence too but you need to be thinking clearly even when she does not need to be thinking clearly," really it is in your best interest to be on top of the game. Why? Because it is your future and your life you could be messing up and it is not up to her to protect you, only you can do that. Like the issue of birth control and condom use, when it comes to consent and sex it is up to you to make sure you are protected.

Protect Yourself

So let's recap quickly:

- Not stopping when she is indicating that she wants you to stop, be it with words, actions or both, is rape. If she seems hesitant don't try to convince her to give in, just stop!

- Just because a girl has had sex with you in the past does not mean she has consented to having sex with you whenever you want it. Forcing the issue could result in you being charged with rape.

- Just because a girl is your girlfriend does not mean she owes you sex on demand. Push it when she doesn't want it and you could be charged with rape.

- If you get a girl drunk or high and then get together with her you have committed a sexual assault. If you do this and then have sex with her it is rape.

- If you do not get a girl drunk or high but you know she is when you have sex you have committed rape.

- If you are unaware that a girl is drunk or high and you have sex with her you could be charged with rape.

- Even if you too are drunk or high when you have sex with a girl who is drunk or high you could be charged with rape. It is not a sufficient defense to say, "I was wasted too!"

Hope that clears up the so-called gray areas on the topic of date rape. Remember it is your responsibility to protect yourself, not only from pregnancy and STDs [sexually transmitted diseases], but also from being charged with date rape. Don't blame your partner for actions you can control. You should use a condom and protect yourself from pregnancy even if she says she is on birth control. You should use a condom to protect yourself from STDs even if she says she is clean. You should stop yourself from having sex when she seems uncomfortable, when she says no, when she physically starts pushing you away or when one or both of you may be intoxicated and protect the both of you from a date rape. It is the right thing to do for EVERYBODY concerned.

Writer's Note: This article is not gender neutral but date rape is. Date rape can and does occur within homosexual relationships and all of the scenarios outlined above apply in these situations as well.

5

The Definition of Rape Has Been Unfairly Changed

Peter Zohrab

Peter Zohrab has written numerous articles defending the equality of men with regard to the feminist movement.

Even during consensual sex, men usually act aggressively and forcefully; therefore, aggression and force do not always constitute rape. And women have been known to say "no" in certain situations in which they actually mean "yes;" therefore, saying "no" does not always constitute rape. Women have changed the definition of date rape so that they can now claim rape whenever they choose, leaving men with no way to defend themselves. The definition of rape needs to be rethought and, to be fair, the issue of male sexuality should be taken into account.

A surprising thing happened to me while working on this book: While I was attending a course for teachers, several Feminists handed me the best disproof of their position on rape I could ever hope to find! In fact, this group (mainly women) is so determinedly Feminist (and left-wing, generally) that I almost had to pinch myself. Here's what happened.

One topic covered during the one-day course was Brain Sex, based on the book of the same name. After talking about a few of the differences between male and female psychology mentioned in that book, the Facilitator, addressing the women in the audience, said something like: "You know what it's like when you tell your husband not to buy you a present for your birthday—and he doesn't?"

Peter Zohrab, *Sex, Lies & Feminism*. Wainuiomata, New Zealand: New Zealand Equity Party, 2002. nzmera.orcon.net.nz. Reproduced by permission.

There was a chorus of patronising agreement from the mainly-female audience. Men are just supposed to know they really do need to buy a gift. So I jumped at the opportunity to say, "That's just like rape. The woman says 'No,' and the man's wrong whatever happens."

There was a surprised, but almost unanimous retort of "No!" from this same audience. (I might have added a man could end up in jail for making one choice in such situations, or lose his marriage if he makes the other choice.)

So, whether a woman says no and means yes in one situation, but says no and means no in another, men are just supposed to magically, telepathically intuit the correct meaning and act accordingly? Only those who benefit from the grant of such whimsy could say this makes sense.

This incident illustrates a number of points: One is that the Feminist insistence a woman always means "No" when she says "No" is a lie, as Camille Paglia [author and university professor], though she calls herself a Feminist, has noted. And many men have gone to jail because that lie has become official doctrine in some courtrooms.

Another point is that allowing only Feminists to have serious input into Sex/Gender policies has created a society in which women can have their cake and eat it too, while men are put into a no-win situation. In other words, western men are increasingly having to choose between avoiding relationships or risking an arrest for rape. A male no-win situation also exists in the area of domestic violence and the divorce courts. Such no-win situations are the inevitable result of institutionalising female pressure-groups, while ignoring and discouraging male pressure-groups, which is what western establishments are doing. . . .

The Anatomical Context of Rape

We can start with the reciprocally non-symmetrical genital anatomy of men and women. Men and women do not have genital anatomy that is reciprocally symmetrical or identical. Instead, they have complementary anatomies.

The crucial elements I want to draw out of the above description are that:

1. the sexual act is a joint endeavour;
2. pressure/force, in most cases, needs to be applied by the man;
3. resistance, in most cases, needs to be applied by the woman.

So we can already see how rape can be a matter of degree. Indeed, far from disagreeing with Feminazis who scream "All Men Are Rapists," I almost agree with them. Men who engage in heterosexual sex are almost compelled to use force against a resisting woman, and that probably comes under many definitions of rape. These facts mean the psychology of an aroused man must typically be very different from the psychology of an aroused woman.

Feminists who scream that rape is not a sexual act but an act of violence are lying, in order to make it more likely that penalties for rape will be increased, and to make the charge of rape harder for a man to defend against in court. The article "The Causes of Criminal Behaviour—why do they do it?" reports that rapists reported urges for sex with an adult woman as a major cause of offending. Any studies that found rape to be the result of anger or a lust for power, need to be reevaluated by researchers who don't have a Feminist axe to grind. Feminists have a strong ideological motive to prove rape is an act of violence, and any "research" carried out by them in this area is bound to have an agenda behind it.

This agenda has gone so far in New Zealand (for example) that the maximum penalty for rape is greater than the maximum penalty for murder! There is a sentence called "preventive detention"—i.e., an indefinite term of incarceration—which is imposed for sex crimes but not for murder, on its own. Here, as in the case of abortion, we find Society values the rights and convenience of women more highly than the life of unborn children or the rights of men. . . .

The Social Context of Rape

The different sexual behaviours of men and women are to some extent isomorphic with their different anatomies. In other words, men have the main tool/weapon of the sex act, and they are also the main initiators of courtship. Women have the receptacle for the sex act, and also tend to be the recipients rather than the initiators of courtship. It is biologically efficient for women to behave generally as passively during courtship as they do during sex itself. Similarly, it is biologically efficient for men to behave generally as aggressively during courtship as they do during the sex act.

This is because both women and men can apply the same sort of mind-set (her: "Let him make the moves"; him: "It's up to me to take the plunge") in both situations. It would be a bit schizophrenic if women made all the moves during courtship then suddenly lapsed into passivity during the sex act itself. In terms of hormones and personality structures, I doubt living beings could evolve in that contradictory sort of way.

Since all men are faced with the necessity of coping with frequent rejection or apparent indifference (and women are not), the survival of the species demands that men adopt a thick-skinned attitude to apparent rejection. The old proverb "hell hath no fury like a woman scorned" only makes sense if women are seldom "scorned." You certainly don't get the impression there are millions of women running around feeling enraged because they were rejected.

Women may well feel rejected at times, in the sense they do not receive the attentions of a man whom they are trying to attract. But that pales in comparison with the frequent experience of men who make (and are expected to make) an overt pass at a woman, who then rejects them crudely and out of hand. There is no proverb such as "hell hath no fury like a man scorned" for the simple reason that being scorned by a woman is an extremely common experience for most men, and they simply couldn't cope with normal life if they went about feeling furious every time this happened.

Women have the luxury of expecting men to make all the moves, then accusing them of rape as and when they wish.

There is also a status issue involved here. You can only get "furious" if you feel you have lost face and been humiliated. For a woman, it is humiliating to expose herself to rejection only to be rejected, whereas a man does not have the sort of status or pride in the context of the mating game that gives him the luxury of feeling humiliated by rejection. He can feel depressed, certainly, but not furious. (In fact, men who do feel enraged by rejection are generally considered very dangerous and potentially criminal.)

Such rejection can be very traumatic at times—especially for adolescent males. So a man has to either put up with celibacy or learn to be thick-skinned. There is only a thin line between such a mentality and the mentality of a rapist, and it is inevitable this boundary will be crossed from time to time. Hence, in the context of defining, recognizing and prosecuting sex crimes, it is grossly unjust to penalise men too harshly for crossing this boundary—particularly while allowing women to behave as they like without running any serious legal risk.

The Legal Concept of Rape

We have to decide whether, or to what extent, rape and female passivity are two sides of the same genetically programmed coin, then design our legal system accordingly. A significant problem is the effect the pervasive Feminist propaganda has, and how it tries to let women have their cake and eat it, too.

Women have the luxury of expecting men to make all the moves, then accusing them of rape as and when they wish.

Masculists should demand sexual equality in the area of sex crimes. The types of crimes women commit should be more heavily penalised than they are at present. To balance the crime of rape (unless it is downgraded in some way), I suggest there should be some legal way of penalising women to an equivalent degree for failing to take the initiative in sexual relationships—or, alternatively, for rejecting a man when it could be argued she "led him on."

In practice and the overwhelming majority of cases, men have to initiate sexual relationships with women in the face of a female attitude ranging from active discouragement (often, but of course not always, turning into acquiescence if the man persists), through to apparent indifference, all the way to ambiguous non-discouragement with possible "signs" of receptivity. One study claims to show that, in singles bars, it is primarily women who initiate sexual relationships. As far as the first actual physical contact is concerned, however, the study apparently included "incidental" or "quasi-accidental" touching of the man by the woman. This would be typical of the general "deniability" stance of women in sexual relationships. Hence, the actual unambiguous, risk-taking transition from casual acquaintance to physical/sexual relationship is still a male responsibility.

What is new about date rape is that it marks an attempted shift in the definition of "rape."

Relatively recently, the concept of "date rape" hit the headlines, particularly in the United States. It resulted in the notorious Antioch College Sexual Offense Prevention Policy (1996), which centres on the following definition of "consent": "the act of willingly and verbally agreeing to engage in specific sexual behavior."

What is new about date rape is that it marks an attempted shift in the definition of "rape." Previously, most people assumed rape was sexual intercourse forced on a woman who stated she was unwilling to participate. With date rape came the idea rape was what a man committed if he had sexual intercourse with a woman who did not explicitly agree to it. This is totally unfair to men. As Thomas [David Thomas wrote *Not Guilty: In Defense of the Modern Man*] (1993) puts it:

> (T)here seems little way in which a boy can avoid being accused of rape. For boys are still expected to take girls out, pour a couple of drinks down them, plead everlasting love and then make a pass. . . . If you don't at least try to seduce them, girls are apt to get offended (and start casting aspersions on your virility—PZ). And . . . there may never be a moment at which anyone actually asks, 'May I?' or gets the answer 'Yes'.

Then there's the old problem of women who say "no" and mean "yes", which I referred to above. Many Feminists deny this ever happens, but Thomas (1993) cites a 1991 poll, conducted among female students at the University of Texas's psychology department, where nearly 50 percent of respondents admitted to saying "no" to sexual advances while really meaning "yes" or "maybe." Most men must be aware of this sort of behaviour from their own experience.

The Political Context of Rape

I find myself in agreement with [columnist and author] Barbara Amiel, who wrote that Feminism. . .

> . . .has moved from the liberal goal of equality between the sexes to the political goal of power for women, and is now well on the road to legislating out of existence the biologically based mating habits of our species. . . . Feminists wish male sexuality to be immaterial in criminal law. Women

should be free to engage in any type of behaviour that suits their own sexuality without regard to the consequences. This approach views men as vibrators: women may pick them up, switch them on, play around and then, if the off-switch doesn't work, sue the manufacturer for damages. . . .

Feminists pooh-pooh the idea any men ever experience such strong urges they literally cannot control themselves. I don't know how they could possibly know this for a fact. Maybe all it means is that women never have such feelings. Certainly a legal system should never require a man to stop intercourse, once started. Nor should a woman have the right to expect a man to control himself to the extent she can tell him to stop once he has actually started the sex-act itself. I assert this as a Men's Rights activist! Men need to have some rights in the sex act, and this needs to be one of them. A man is not merely a living vibrator at a woman's beck and call. He cannot be just switched on and off as it happens to suit some woman and the anti-male Legal System. . . .

The issue of rape needs to be rethought in western societies. As with other Men's/Fathers' Issues, there should be—and probably will be—a two-pronged assault on the status quo:

1. Specialist groups of men will concentrate on lobbying for specific law changes.

2. Generalist Men's Rights activists will gradually make society realise that the feelings, interests and rights of men and fathers need to be taken into account when legislative and administrative decisions are made that affect them. This will gradually apply to laws relating to rape as well as to other parts of the legal system.

In this context, the customs of societies where women make an effort to be modest and to keep themselves hidden from unrelated men no longer seem very strange. They are one solution to an age-old problem. Modern Feminist societies have taken the line that women can "have it all"—i.e., if something goes wrong, the blame is put squarely on the man. That is unfair on men.

If something goes wrong, the blame is put squarely on the man.

I see no obvious utopia, as far as the law on rape is concerned. Rape is a problem. Part of the problem is that the law is intervening in the areas of courtship and the sex act, and these areas do not put the same pressures onto both men and women. For now, I suggest only that we think beyond and around the "Woman as Goddess-Victim" mindset we are suffering from at present.

6

The Definition of Rape Has Been Duly Clarified

Sherry F. Colb

Sherry F. Colb is a professor at Rutgers Law School in Newark, New Jersey.

An important consideration regarding the legal definition of rape is the issue of consent. Many state courts have held that once consent has been given, it may not be withdrawn later during the encounter. However, in January 2003, the California Supreme Court ruled that regardless of initial consent, whenever a woman (or a man) tells her partner to stop, and he forces her to continue, rape has occurred. When sex is forced—at any time during the encounter—it is rape, and now it will be duly punished as such.

Earlier this month [January 2003], the Supreme Court of California confronted an important issue about how rape should be defined under the law. In *People v. John Z.*, the court held that a woman who initially consents to sexual intercourse does not thereby give up her right to end the encounter at whatever point she chooses. In other words, when a woman tells her partner to stop, and he forces her to continue, he is guilty of rape.

One could imagine difficult factual variations, in which the woman's communication is ambiguous or her partner's compliance almost, but not quite, immediate. The basic ruling, however, should not be controversial. If a woman (or a

Sherry F. Colb, "Withdrawing Consent During Intercourse: California's Highest Court Clarifies the Definition of Rape," Findlaw.com, January 15, 2003. Reproduced by permission.

man, for that matter) is clear in conveying the desire to end a sexual interaction, a decision forcibly to disregard that desire is an instance of rape.

Of greater interest than the California court's decision itself, is the fact that the court took the case in order to resolve a lower court split over the issue. According to at least one court in the state of California, then, for purposes of rape law, consent to penetration—once given—may not be withdrawn. And courts in other states have held the same.

Such a position rests on outdated ideas about the harm of rape and the biological imperatives of men who are engaged in sexual intercourse.

An Old View of the Harm of Rape

In *People v. Vela*—one of the cases the Supreme Court overruled with its recent decision—a California appellate court had held that as long as an alleged victim gives consent prior to penetration, there is no rape, despite the withdrawal of consent during intercourse.

The *Vela* court cited precedents from Maryland and North Carolina as persuasive authority. (Of course, out-of-state cases do not bind California courts, but California courts may nonetheless be swayed by their analysis). The majority reasoned that

> "the essence of the crime of rape is the outrage to the person and feelings of the female resulting from the nonconsensual violation of her womanhood. . . . If [after consenting to penetration,] she withdraws consent during the act of sexual intercourse, and the male forcibly continues the act without interruption. . . the sense of outrage to her person and feelings could hardly be of the same magnitude [as would the disregard of an initial refusal]. . . ."

Though the court speaks of the woman's person and feelings, its use of the words "violation of her womanhood" evokes an earlier century—a time when a woman who was no longer "intact" would have much less cause to feel violated by rape than her purer sister. The court's argument, then, suggests a continuum of harms, one in which sex without consent is in some instances very bad; in some, not so bad; and in some, perfectly fine.

Juries today remain skeptical about a woman's claims of rape if she is "promiscuous."

Consider the greatest "outrage" along the *Vela* court's implicit scale. The virgin who has saved herself for her wedding night has the strongest interest in avoiding unwanted intercourse. Her purity as a maiden hangs in the balance, and any man who would disregard that purity commits a grave offense against her and her family. Indeed, in the Bible, a man who rapes a virgin is said to owe her father damages and is expected to marry his victim. In that way, presumably, he can ensure that her reduced market value does not eliminate her prospects for marriage and a family.

In modern secular cultures, by contrast, non-virgins also have the right not to be raped. And, of course, a rapist cannot avoid liability for his crime through marriage.

Nonetheless, juries today remain skeptical about a woman's claims of rape if she is "promiscuous"—a vestige of the notion that a woman has one opportunity to decide whether she will be a good girl who waits until she is married or a bad girl who doesn't. As soon as she says "yes" once, she's "that kind of girl" forever.

The crime of rape, on this account, has more to do with a victim's character or "virtue"—her status, that is—than with her right to bodily integrity against all manner of sexual intrusion.

The Marital Rape Exemption: Another Relic

Even if one progresses beyond a status approach to the definition of a rape victim, one might nonetheless believe that with respect to any one man, a woman who says "yes" forfeits her right to say no forever after. This, after all, is the perspective of marital rape exemptions. Only a few decades ago, these exemptions permitted men in much of the country to force their wives to have intercourse without criminal accountability for rape. (Many jurisdictions, moreover, continue to rank marital rape as a less serious offense than the rape of a stranger).

A progenitor of the marital rape exemption in this country was Sir Matthew Hale, a former Chief Justice in England. When British practices were imported to the U.S., Hale's view on marital rape came along. Hale famously said in the eighteenth century that "the husband cannot be guilty of a rape committed by himself upon his lawful wife, for by their mutual matrimonial consent and contract the wife hath given up herself in this kind unto her husband, which she cannot retract."

Some even argued in the late twentieth century for extension of the marital rape exemption to cohabitants. The argument was that limiting the rape license to married men was unfair to unmarried men who have undertaken committed, monogamous relationships that should entitle them to the same sexual access to their women as married men have to theirs. A number of states—including Connecticut, Kentucky, and Pennsylvania—apparently found such reasoning convincing, for they embodied it in their laws.

On this theory of rape, a woman may decide which men have and do not have consent, but once that initial decision is made, she cannot pick and choose on which occasions those men may exercise their prerogative. Consent thus becomes something like an unrestricted train pass on Amtrak.

Under such a view, the logic of *Vela* is / woman who not only has chosen to consen/ man but has consented to him *in the very same em* necessarily given up any right to stop him. She may stu. able to decide to say no to some men (and perhaps even to decide on any given day whether to say yes *again,* to a man with whom she has been intimate before). But if consensual penetration has already taken place, she must live with her decision, a variation on the expression, "you've made your bed; now lie in it."

An Enlightened View

One might understand the harm of rape very differently, however. On this alternative understanding, what is wrong with rape is that it compels a person to be subjected to sexual intercourse, when she has specifically and clearly indicated that she does not want to be.

She may choose to say "stop it" for any of a variety of reasons. Perhaps the particular man is unattractive to her, or she is not in the mood to have sex, or maybe she has an infection that unexpectedly renders the particular experience physically painful. Regardless of her reasons, though, the consent is hers to give or take away, on any particular occasion, as she so chooses.

This view takes account of an emotional reality: Regardless of what motivates a particular woman to refuse a man, his deliberate, forcible disregard of that refusal is a traumatizing and humiliating experience for her. It inflicts harm because it takes a decision about the most intimate, personal, and vulnerable matters in her life out of a woman's hands.

The giving of consent . . . should not be [irrevocable].

The harm of rape, then, is in forcibly depriving a person of her right of bodily integrity. The marital rapist—or any

43

rapist who has once received consent—still violates the woman, because he treats her earlier consent as a transfer of dominion instead of an expression of desire that—to be freely given—must be freely revocable as well.

The Problem with a "Waiver" Approach to Consent

Not only does the *Vela* approach to sexual consent reflect a regressive view of women's sexuality, but it is also troubling for a second reason: It treats consent as the moral equivalent of a "waiver."

In legal parlance, "waiver" refers to a situation in which a person voluntarily decides to give up a right that he has. A defendant charged with a crime, for example, has the right to a trial. If he pleads guilty, he waives that right and thereby foregoes the benefits that a trial would have accorded him. He cannot later, after sentencing, decide that he would like to have a trial after all.

Similarly, a defendant who goes to trial has a Fifth Amendment right to refuse to take the witness stand. She may decide nonetheless to testify in her own behalf. But by doing so, she waives her Fifth Amendment right not to be compelled to answer a prosecutor's questions (at least those that fall within the scope of her direct examination).

In these situations, the person who has waived her rights has given them up and ordinarily cannot later decide to reassert them. The waiver, in other words, is irrevocable. The giving of consent, however, should not be.

Almost by definition, an assertion that "I don't want to do this anymore" negates an earlier consent. The reason that waivers are not always revocable is that the party who has obtained the waiver may develop an interest in relying on that waiver, because the party has reciprocally given up something valuable as well.

When a defendant takes the witness stand and waives her Fifth Amendment rights, for example, she provides the jury with evidence that the prosecutor now has an interest in rebutting, an interest that was not present prior to the defendant's testifying. It would accordingly be unfair to deny the prosecutor an opportunity for cross-examination under these circumstances.

The Myth of the Unstoppable Male

Should consent to sexual intercourse be treated as an irrevocable waiver? Those who argue in the affirmative believe that a man who has received consent will properly allow his biological urges to take over, in a way that makes it unfair to demand of him that he stop. He has, in other words, relinquished his obligation to exercise self-control, in response to the woman's invitation.

As the brief in support of the defendant in *John Z.* put it, "[b]y essence of the act of sexual intercourse, a male's primal urge to reproduce is aroused. It is therefore unreasonable for a female and the law to expect a male to cease having sexual intercourse immediately upon her withdrawal of consent."

Giving legal protection to a male's unstoppable "primal urge" treats the man's sexual desire as a bullet that—once fired—is physically impossible to stop. This view has significant implications for women's safety and liberty.

Taken to its logical conclusion, such an approach requires women to restrict their behaviors in all sorts of ways—including how they dress and whether they appear in public unescorted—if they are to avoid being sexually assaulted. It removes male accountability for sexual assault and instead places responsibility upon the woman to prove that she took all possible steps to avoid awakening the man's primal urge.

Just like the status definition of the harm of rape (suggesting that rape only counts when it happens to virgins and not to the "promiscuous"), the myth of the unstoppable male effectively regulates women in the guise of defining sexual assault. In fact, it may be precisely the desire to dominate and punish a woman who has behaved like a "tease" that motivates men to force them to continue to have sex after consent has been unambiguously withdrawn. In that sense, the sexual act that proceeds after a woman's withdrawal of consent is no longer truly the "same" act as that which took place while her partner still had consent.

That puts the law to a choice: It must either punish aroused men who inflict forcible intercourse, or condone the violent punishment of fickle women who frustrate the "primal urge."

No Means No, Whenever and to Whomever It Is Said

Many of us are loath to regulate intimacy. Some of my readers may even remember the infamous Antioch Code, in which male college students were expected to ask female companions' permission for each advancing stage of intimacy in a sexual encounter. Comedians had a field day with the Antioch Code, including sketches in which a male would say, "May I now escalate our level of intimacy by moving my lips from your neck to your ear?"

In a democracy, it would seem, consenting adults should generally be free to engage in sexual relationships without government oversight or instructions on how to escalate intimacy. That being said, however, the reality of consent is a crucial precondition to such freedom. The liberty to harm another is not, and should not be, protected.

Freedom thus requires that consent not be presumed or irrevocable—but actual and true. So that women may decide whether or not to have or to continue to have sex, then, free men must be capable of resisting primal urges, no matter how strong or at what point they emerge. Those men who cannot or will not do so are sexual predators and should be legally recognized as such.

7

Date Rapists Should Be Severely Prosecuted

Katherine Eastvold

Katherine Eastvold maintains the Eastvold Blog, *in which she writes about current events.*

Rapists come in many different personifications: adults, college students, child predators, and even young men out on dates. Who they are or where they come from does not alter the fact that they committed rape, which is a serious crime. If the perpetrator is a regular guy from a nice family, it is unfortunate that he will have to live with the stigma of being labeled a sex offender for the rest of his life. But a victim of rape must live with the devastating consequences of that rape, and so should the rapist.

Columnist Kathleen Parker is on a crusade to convince people to think differently about one category of convicted rapists—namely, young college men accused of date rape in situations where alcohol and/or drugs were involved. . . .

Her legal/political argument is that men accused of date rape (she seems particularly concerned for young men who commit their crime in college, particularly under the influence; I'm not sure how she would feel about older, less seemingly innocent date rape perpetrators) should not be subjected to the same lengthy sentences and burdensome restrictions as other rapists. As she put it in today's [May 10, 2006] column,

Katherine Eastvold, "Rape Is Always Wrong," The Eastvold Blog, May 11, 2006. Reproduced by permission.

"sex offenders" and "sex predators" are not the same thing. A sex predator, as she describes it, is the kind of guy who kidnaps an 8-year-old girl, brutally rapes and murders her, and cuts the body up into a bunch of gruesome pieces. Probably not the kind of guy you want living next door. A sex offender, on the other hand, could be the proverbial "guy next door"—a good kid who played football, went to college, and made a little mistake while drunk at a frat party. Her question: do we really want to ruin this guy's life by putting him on sex offender registries, alerting his potential neighbors and employers, etc.?

Of course I agree that there's a huge difference between Parker's description of a sex predator and her description of a typical date rapist. Of course the former is more dangerous than the latter; he is more likely to be a repeat offender, precisely because he probably has a serious mental/emotional disturbance. (I say that as a matter of fact, not at all to excuse his actions.) So, as a practical matter, Parker is right; there are very good reasons to keep convicted "predators" (particularly those who have targeted children, the handicapped, and other vulnerable populations) on a short leash once they're released from prison, whereas the same precautions might be unnecessary to keep a date rapist from striking again. However, Parker ignores two important facts: first, the predator she describes is not just a rapist, but a murderer, and he has targeted a victim who is legally incapable of consent. These are more serious crimes than rape, and they are already treated as such by our court system. Secondly, her portrait of the typical date rapist does not describe every date rapist. Not all date rapes involve alcohol or drugs, and many, many date rapes involve a victim who is considerably more intoxicated than the perpetrator. Many date rapists are older men, not impressionable college kids making a mistake. To assert that date rape, across the board, is a crime of mere irresponsibility (if even that) is itself irresponsible. Some date rapists may, in fact, be very likely to offend again, and the courts need to have the option of continued surveillance after release.

Date Rape Should Not Be Excused

What concerns me even more than the legal question, though, is Parker's attempt to make us feel so sorry for young men in this situation—reentering society, after a number of years in prison, with the burden of the "sex offender" label—as to excuse their behavior. She is especially fond of bringing up Rich Gorman, a junior business/computing major at Florida State University who is serving five years behind bars for allegedly having sex with a fellow student (Parker rather visciously decides to call her "Chastity") after she told him to stop. They went to her apartment after a party, and she had been drinking. (There doesn't seem to be any evidence that Gorman was drinking or had his judgment otherwise impaired; in today's column, Parker simply calls him "confused.")

It's not any less of a crime because the perpetrator was drunk or confused or immature or a "good college Joe" who comes from a nice family and makes good grades.

Parker describes Gorman as "a regular college Joe, a good student and a good son," but dredges up "Chastity"'s drug problems, the fact that she had a new boyfriend and was back at campus parties soon after the accusation, and the fact that she had previously accused another student of rape under similar circumstances. She laments that "one life goes on" while "the other is ruined" (Gorman will be on probation until he is 37 and under sex offender restrictions until he is 47.) Never mind that a drug habit and living with the knowledge that she has falsely accused two men (if Parker is correct) doesn't sound like a very nice life to me, whereas at least Gorman (if he is innocent) will sleep the sleep of the just.

But never mind the particulars of this case. I am seriously concerned and offended by this latest attempt to discredit women who dare to report rapes, and to make men who have sex with drunk women into "nice people." Yes, it's a serious burden to have to constantly explain to potential employers why you're on the sex offender registry, or to put up with hostile stares from neighbors. Yes, women are not always helpless victims, and they do sometimes lie and make false accusations in a very badly wrong attempt to deal with pain and regret the morning after a bad decision. (But then again, that's what jury trials are for; hopefully, most of the time, a trial will reveal inconsistencies in a false victim's story, and the jury will vote to acquit.) But a man (yes, 22 is young, but a 22-year-old is expected to act like a man and take responsibility like a man in this society) should think about these things before he has sex with a woman who is drunk or high. Call me a prude, but maybe he should think about these consequences (along with a host of others) before having sex with any woman outside marriage.

Rape is real. And it's a crime. It's not any less of a crime because the perpetrator was drunk or confused or immature or a "good college Joe" who comes from a nice family and makes good grades. It has real, devastating consequences for the victim. And it should be punished. We can feel sorry for men living with the sex offender stigma, but our sympathy shouldn't keep us from insisting they pay reasonable consequences for their actions.

8

Date Rape Drugging Is Widespread in the Queer Community

Zak Szymanski

Zak Szymanski is assistant editor at the Bay Area Reporter *and co-coordinator of the queer youth column.*

The use of date rape drugs in gay bars is on the rise. Drugging has received mainstream attention for heterosexuals, but getting victims of sexual assault in the queer community to report their attacks has not been easy. Often if the victim is queer, he or she has a difficult time getting adequate medical, law enforcement, and legal help. And the fact that drugging victims cannot remember the event or provide witnesses further complicates the documentation of theses crimes. Queers may not be at greater risk than heterosexuals for drug-related sexual assaults, but considering that they are often targeted for hate crimes because of their sexual orientation, they are at least equally at risk and should be alert to the problem.

"Woman Raped After Leaving Bar," the April [2003] announcement declared, following an alleged incident outside a lesbian-frequented San Francisco dance club known for its mixed LGBT [Lesbian, Gay, Bisexual, and Transgender] crowd. A visitor to the city reported that after feeling sick and trying to hail a cab, three men accosted her, took her to an unknown location and sexually assaulted her for several hours, all the while using antilesbian slurs.

Zak Szymanski, "Dangerous Mix," *Curve*, November 2003. Reproduced by permission.

The public alert was issued by a local agency, Community United Against Violence (CUAV), a nonprofit organization that tracks hate crimes and domestic abuse within queer communities. But the alleged rape was downplayed by the media, including the gay press, because reporters were suspicious of the victim's account.

According to police, the victim was unable to pay a hotel bill, and officers were called in to address the situation. When questioned, the victim incoherently described being assaulted—and apparently robbed—the previous night, but couldn't remember most of the details.

To some, this story sounded like an on-the-spot excuse for getting out of a sticky situation. But to groups like CUAV and fellow member organizations that make up the LGBT-specific National Coalition of Anti-Violence Programs (NCAVP), the victim's story was all too typical of an underreported crime within LGBT circles: assault and/or robbery as a result of involuntary drugging.

Whether dropped into a drink or disguised as a recreational substance, the use of so-called "date-rape drugs" in gay bars is on the rise, according to Avy Skolnik, direct services coordinator of the Colorado Anti-Violence Program. Queer sexual assaults as a result of involuntary drugging experienced a statistical climb in the Denver area at the beginning of 2003, prompting his agency to draft an article for the local gay newspaper.

"We have seen a recent spike in the number of calls we receive from people reporting a sexual assault of which they have no recollection," stated his piece, "Date Rape Drugs: Not Just a Straight Thing," which ran in the newspaper *Out Front Colorado.* "Victims wake up usually feeling sore and remembering some events of the night before, but knowing that at some point, they blacked out. This is usually puzzling because the victim doesn't recall drinking enough to result in a blackout."

Characteristics of Date Rape Drugs

A date-rape drug can actually be any substance that induces unconsciousness, although the drugs most often used for malicious purposes include GHB [Gamma hydroxybutyrate], Ketamine, and Rohypnol.

Such drugs are dangerous for several reasons, according to DanceSafe, a national project dedicated to reducing harm within nightclub environments: They are often colorless and odorless, making them easy to disguise in drinks and as part of other drugs; they take effect quickly, causing a variety of physical symptoms, including blackouts and memory loss; they impair judgment, and may even make users more sexually aroused; and they can exit the body within a matter of days, leaving no evidence that such a drugging ever occurred. In short, they are a sexual predator's dream.

"People may seem more attractive or interesting while under the influence of a drug. Taking drugs may also lead to a loss of inhibitions. You may act more confident than usual and find yourself in situations that wouldn't normally arise," according to a DanceSafe statement geared toward recreational users of the same substances.

These drugs also can be life-threatening, particularly when mixed with alcohol, and can cause extremely low blood pressure and heart rate, temporary coma, or death. A person who succumbs to the intended effects of a date-rape drug is already in danger, as DanceSafe notes that unconsciousness is often the result of an overdose.

Date-rape drugs have received widespread mainstream attention, with coverage that conjures up an image of a straight man forcing his female companion to comply with his sexual demands. Yet LGBT advocates caution that such drugs are also the weapons of hate, and they make their ensuing attacks difficult to report, track and classify, particularly within the queer community.

"It's already hard enough for a victim to prove in the legal system that a sexual assault occurred," says Tina D'Elia, hate violence survivor advocate at CUAV. "If that victim is queer, most likely s/he also has a difficult time receiving adequate medical, police and legal help. And if there was a drugging involved, you're likely dealing with no witnesses, very little recollection of the event and a good chance that the drug is already gone from the victim's system. These very specific types of crimes are extremely difficult to document and successfully prosecute."

No Accurate Count

There is currently no solid data on queer sexual assaults as a result of drugging. Only within the last several months have the member agencies of NCAVP added a drugging category to their crisis intake forms, a move that reflects how such crimes are now on the LGBT community's radar.

It's almost impossible that a person's sexual orientation does not become an issue during a rape.

Making matters more difficult is how—and where—such crimes get reported. Most victims who report drugging-related sexual assaults to LGBT-specific agencies are gay men and transgendered women. But such agencies caution that a lack of information on lesbian and female-born queer victims does not mean such populations aren't being targeted.

LGBT organizations may already be at a disadvantage when it comes to identifying female victims, because many women have rape-crisis centers available to them that don't necessarily document their victims' sexual orientation. Advocates and counselors say that the mainstream system tends to treat assaults upon lesbians or bisexual women raped by men similarly to assaults upon straight women who are raped by men.

More complex is the nature of such reporting. LGBT victims may not know how to classify the crime committed against them, often because of the fuzzy line between a "date" and a "stranger," particularly in a culture centered around the bar scene. If the perpetrator was a bar pickup, date, or familiar face within an already small community, a victim may view the incident as partner violence, and advocates say victims are very reluctant to report sexual assault within the context of dating, particularly if it requires disclosing their sexual orientation to authorities.

Sexual Assaults as Hate Crimes

But sexual assault can take many forms, note LGBT advocates, and they can often occupy more than one criminal category.

"There's not a clear line between date rape and stranger assault," says D'Elia, who points out that statistically, 60–80 percent of sexual assaults are committed by someone the victim knows. "Sexual assault is an interesting thing. It could be a hate crime, or it could be the start of an abusive relationship."

Just because the assailant was a date, say advocates, doesn't mean there weren't ill intentions all along. And such intentions coupled with any type of bias could classify the assault as a hate crime.

"One of the things we've been trying to push the public to acknowledge is that it's almost impossible that a person's sexual orientation does not become an issue during a rape," says Rachel Baum, associate director of the New York-based NCAVP. "When queers are targeted for sexual violence, it is often to 'teach them a lesson,' and assailants are targeting the one thing that is the object of their hatred: the victim's genitalia or sexuality."

Traditionally, notes NCAVP's Skolnik, any rape against a biological woman by a biological man is treated by his agency as a hate crime, considering the historical power imbalance and specific gender and sex factors that go into targeting the victim. A female victim's sexual orientation may then be looked at as an additional reason for the attack.

But LGBT hatred isn't limited to heterosexual male suspects in cases of assault, he says, which is often overlooked. Law enforcement dealing with a queer-on-queer assault may see both parties as "gay," forgetting the hatred that can exist within the queer community toward racial minorities, women and transgenders.

If the perpetrator was a partner or acquaintance, there's a taboo around acknowledging that kind of violence within the lesbian community.

"Just because both the perpetrator and victim are queer," says Skolnik, "doesn't mean it wasn't a hate crime."

Further complicating the documentation of drugging crimes, says Skolnik, is that victims who can't remember the event have very little recourse within the system.

"When a victim has no recollection of the assault, even when there's been physical evidence such as bruises and/or damaged clothing, if they didn't get tested in time for one of these drugs, then police won't even take a report," says Skolnik. "It's a big problem."

D'Elia, like many LGBT advocates, is frustrated by the lack of funding and resources dedicated to tracking queer violence. And while she believes that NCAVP's new intake forms will help identify trends in crimes accompanied by drugging, her gut feeling is that "there's a gap" when it comes to tracking queer female victims of such crimes.

"There are so many reasons why we may not be getting the full picture around these victims of crimes involving drugging," says D'Elia. "There is already shame around reporting sexual assaults. Sometimes the shame and fear can increase if the victim also has to report something like her sexuality, voluntary drug use or underage drinking. And if the perpetrator was a partner or acquaintance, there's a taboo around acknowledging that kind of violence within the lesbian community."

Drugging for the Fun of It

Although advocates believe most drugging-related crimes are accompanied by an attempted or successful rape and/or robbery, sometimes the perpetrator's assault is limited simply to spiking a victim's drink.

Jamie Johnston, who lives in New York City, was vacationing in a nearby resort town last May when she and a group of friends decided to attend a dance club known for its gay circuit parties. The environment was "electric, trancelike and very sweaty," says Johnston, who adds that several times during the evening she was offered drugs by people she had just met. She stuck to her vodka-cranberry and a few cigarettes outside the bar's main entrance.

Being in a queer space felt safe to Johnston, but perhaps it shouldn't have: After leaving and returning to her drink several times, she began to feel nauseated and dizzy. Her next memories consist of drifting in and out of consciousness in her hotel room while her friends watched over her. Only upon her return home did she hear that the same nightclub was the scene of a GHB overdose by a man who, friends said, never touched drugs.

"Suddenly that night kind of made sense to me," says Johnston, who believes she was the victim of a forced party atmosphere rather than a possible target for assault. "People were pretty into making sure that everyone was getting high."

Johnston makes no assumptions about who may have drugged her drink, as the crowd was mixed and she couldn't always tell who was a regular and who was a tourist. "Either way, I made the mistake of believing that gays wouldn't hurt each other, or that outsiders wouldn't dare mess with gay space," she says. "Well, somebody did."

Johnston's story comes as no surprise to Allison Burgos, a club producer and promoter in Miami known for her popular gatherings, such as Girls in Wonderland. Burgos has taken to warning all her patrons to watch their drinks ever since a male friend strolled over to a neighborhood gay bar for a leisurely Sunday afternoon cocktail. "Somebody put something in his drink, and he had a negative reaction to it," Burgos explains. "They found him unconscious in his living room. That was two years ago, and he still hasn't woken up [from his coma]."

Although Burgos sees less drug use within the lesbian community, she does not see dyke-on-dyke drugging as an impossibility.

"I'm always very careful not to leave my drink unattended, and that's in any club—gay, straight or lesbian. I don't drink or use drugs, but I've had people who really wanted me to, and have almost tried to force me," she says. "Sometimes, drugging is not necessarily a means to an end. Sometimes the motivation may be just that someone has a sick sense of humor."

Rules to Live By

The false sense of security of being in LGBT space can be just the environment a potential attacker may be banking on, says D'Elia, who two years ago actually made such an announcement while emceeing the San Francisco Dyke March.

"We basically announced that everyone should be watching their drinks, that the playful and uninhibited atmosphere could put people at risk," she says.

Avoiding danger includes keeping drinks close by—even water. Other rules, according to Skolnik, include not accepting unopened drinks from others (sealed cans and bottles are OK); always having a trusted friend nearby; and avoiding punch bowls at parties.

If an assault and/or drugging does occur, says Skolnik, seek medical attention and ask to be tested for Rohypnol, GHB and Ketamine. And remember that consenting to sex is an active response—or should be, at least.

"One cannot consent to sex when one is in fear, intoxicated or under the influence of the above-mentioned drugs," he says.

By no means is any LGBT agency suggesting that queers are at greater risk for drugging-related assaults. But Baum cautions that continuing to view drugging, date rape and sexual assault as heterosexual phenomena can be dangerous.

"It's not less of an issue because we're queer," says Baum. "At times, we may be at an even greater risk of sexual assault because we are targeted for our sexual orientation or gender identity. We are certainly not at a lower risk than heterosexuals."

9

Campus Feminists Provoke False Rape Accusations

David R. Usher

David R. Usher is president of the American Coalition for Fathers and Children, Missouri coalition.

Feminists have become extremely influential on college and university campuses and have devised a productive method of male-bashing: teach women to use sex to take advantage of men. Take, for example, the 2006 story about members of the men's lacrosse team at North Carolina's Duke University raping a stripper. The accuser certainly did not behave like a rape victim, and there was no physical evidence to prove a rape occurred, yet the campus feminists insisted that charges be filed. After all, false rape accusations often lead to civil suits, which can result in financial gain for the alleged victim. To protect their finances and reputations, men need to take back control from the feminists and insist on equal rights.

When the story broke [in 2006] about the Men's lacrosse team at Duke University raping a black stripper, it reminded me of the many legendary false child abuse cases of the 1970's and 1980's.

The story did not ring true to begin with. Rapists sneak around and do things as anonymously as possible. They plan their mark and then police spend a lot of time and resources to figure out who did it. Gang-raping women in busy college party bathrooms while hollering racial epithets is not something that happens even at "Animal House."

David R. Usher, "The Hazards of Duke: Predatory Feminism," OpinionEditorials.com, May 1, 2006. Reproduced by permission.

Photographic evidence in the possession of the defense apparently shows that the alleged victim was already "substantially impaired" (a gentlemanly euphemism for "smashed"). Upon arriving, she already had numerous scrapes on her legs and knees from falling down.

The "suspicious" email sent by one of the alleged rapists did not add up either. Folks do not send emails to friends joking nervously about torturing and killing a stripper unless something very upsetting did indeed take place—a disagreement over paying a stripper too impaired to perform.

The victim claims she left the party early out of fear. But she returned later, with more photos recording "a major grin on her face." She never mentioned rape to her stripper friend, either.

Does any of this look like a case of rape? No. Does it look like a publicity stunt to make a lot of money in a civil suit and book deal? Yes.

Lack of Evidence

We know that there was no DNA evidence anywhere on the stripper's body. She was swabbed head-to-toe and nothing matched. If a woman was gang-raped and clawed the arm of her attacker, the chance of doing so without somebody leaving even one strand of DNA on her is about zero. In fact, this essentially proves that none of the 46 white members of the team even touched her!

The complete lack of DNA evidence proves the claims in the probable-cause search warrant affidavit are ridiculous. It would be virtually impossible not to have some DNA evidence given the specific physical interactions alleged by our stripper: "The three males (Adam, Brett, and Matt) forcefully held her legs and arms and raped and sexually assaulted her anally, vaginally, and orally" . . . "the victim stated she was hit, kicked, and strangled during the assault" . . . "she claimed she was clawing at one of the suspect's arms in an attempt to breathe while being strangled."

The evidence collected indicates that the criminal case will fail. It is not possible to reach a conclusion "beyond reasonable doubt" in a trial where the prosecution's case rests on anecdotal tea-leaf reading.

Eager to Accuse

District Attorney Mike Nifong said that "medical exams performed on the woman showed injuries consistent with rape and emotional trauma." The word "consistent" is a catchphrase often used by abuse validators. It means everything and nothing at the same time. Abuse validators adopted this technique out of necessity: when you are on contract to government, and you do not regularly produce the results it is looking for, it takes the contract elsewhere.

Rape and child abuse trauma centers consistently produce findings consistent with the allegations. For example, in one notorious St. Louis court case, Dr. Montaleone, Director of Cardinal Glennon Hospital's trauma center testified on cross-examination: "You can never say that a child has not been abused. Never."

Colleges . . . teach women how to use sex to take advantage of men and any institution that involves men.

Trauma centers are often magnets for people-savers who believe there is abuse hiding under every rock. It is known that many of these individuals were abused themselves. They are unlikely to approach cases scientifically.

Nifong is risking his political career trying to make milk from manure. He is up for election in May. We have seen shotgun sex and race prosecutions backfire before. Nifong shouldn't worry about losing. His qualifications as a trash collector make him a shoo-in for a job driving a city garbage truck.

This is exactly what the University deserves for allowing feminists to run the campus in the first place, while stifling the healthy political and social views of heterosexual men. Organized feminism is about women and trial lawyers using sex to make money from a pedestal of feigned Victorian purity. And, Duke has about as much money as the state of North Carolina has.

The classic false child abuse cases of the 1970's and 1980's such as McMartin and Little Rascals had two things in common: the stories did not remotely match the realities, and the litigants were highly motivated by the foreknown scent of huge civil suit settlements. Feminists discovered that these cases often backfired because it is difficult to brainwash children. In the late-1980's, feminists decided that false rape and spousal abuse allegations are much safer and more productive methods to take over marriages, hit the civil jackpot, and wipe out religion and sports teams. It worked very well until new DNA science methodology came along to ruin the ruse. Now states have thousands of falsely-incarcerated men and a lot of cases to retry at tremendous expense to taxpayers.

Influence of Campus Feminists

Our stripper is a student at a North Carolina Central University. Colleges are famous for mandatory hyper-feminist coursework featuring lawyers and feminist activists that teach women how to use sex to take advantage of men and any institution that involves men.

NCCU has a chapter of the National Organization for Women on campus. One of its major "missions" is fostering the agitprop on which the Violence Against Women Act (VAWA) is based—to keep $4-billion in sexist VAWA federal funding flowing. As many of us know, VAWA is a dangerous program using vivid sexual allegory to distract from the fact that women cause just as much domestic violence as men do. Campus feminists love VAWA because it provides lots of play money for misuse pushing the full scope of feminist initiatives, including lesbian marriage, abortion, and generic hate of men. Why Congress funds these deeply sexist political initiatives with our tax dollars is a serious question for the upcoming elections.

NCCU is an extension of Duke, which has an extensive women's studies department tentacled deeply into core curricula via its funded interdisciplinary studies program. Duke has a fully-integrated SASS chapter (that screams out all sorts of social statistics debunked long ago) and a Center for LGBT [Lesbian, Gay, Bisexual, and Transgender] Life (complete with their own "lavender graduation ceremonies").

The mission statement of Duke's women's studies program is nothing short of an end-stage fascist manifesto expressing full intent to turn all core curricula into subdivisions of feminist dicta:

> In the field's first decades, feminist scholarship reoriented traditional disciplines toward the study of women and gender and developed new methodologies and critical vocabularies that have made interdisciplinarity a key feature of Women's Studies as an autonomous field. Today, scholars continue to explore the meaning and impact of identity as a primary—though by no means transhistorical or universal—way of organizing social life by pursuing an intersectional analysis of gender, race, sexuality, class, and nationality. In the classroom, as in our research, our goal is to transform the university's organization of knowledge by reaching across the epistemological and methodological divisions of historical, political, economic, representational, technological and scientific analysis. In our Program's dual emphasis on interdisciplinarity and intersectionality, we offer students new knowledge about identity while equipping them with a wide range of analytical and methodological skill.

But UNC and Duke, like most universities, do not have men's studies programs. This is because "professional" feminism dictates that men are not allowed to have views on social issues, marriage, family, divorce, childbearing, or childrearing. The feminist idea of equality: women must have equal rights to be in the workplace, but men should not have any right to be in the family or to even think about it. Such is the situation of men at Duke.

But don't take my word for this. A 1965 graduate of Duke noticed a feminist problem there too:

> When this is all over, the team should demand and receive apologies from Duke's president and the local 'activists' who naturally assumed the worst, although no formal charges had or have been made. Further, the team should receive compensation for damages to individual and team reputations. Finally, the University should mandate a refresher course in constitutional rights for its faculty and students. That said, having observed the decided tilt to the left at Duke over the last three decades, I'd encourage the team not to hold its collective breath.—*Daniel (Duke '65)*

My recommendation to Duke: When they file the civil suit, do not back down. File a countersuit against the woman and the local abuse center for double the amount they are asking. You cannot stop the Pink Mafia by paying it off.

Equal Rights for Men

My message to men and real women on college campuses everywhere: Stay away from feminists and strippers. The last thing you want to date is a girl who studies feminism. Be sure she believes in equal rights for men to be in the family. Make certain she rejects feminism before even asking her out on a date. Get to know her previous boyfriend to find out why they broke up. If she says he is a jerk but he isn't, you probably have a feminist on your hands.

Start a men's rights group on your campus. Insist on equal rights for normal heterosexual men to be politically organized and to have their views on social equality heard. Demand the creation of a men's studies program that operates completely independently of the women's studies department. Real women will support you in this. Be sure to include them in your work.

The Duke board of directors should be more than happy to have you restore balance on campus to prevent feminists from manufacturing future assaults on Duke's finances and reputation.

All social change starts on college campuses. This is precisely why feminists have entrenched themselves into powerful positions controlling all campus social thought. This will not be an easy task, but it will be the best education that any man can possibly get in politics.

It is far better to deal with feminism at the political level now and change your future than it is to wait for your own social and economic destruction later.

Feminism has already destroyed over half the husbands and fathers in America. What you fail to do now is what you will get later.

10

Campus Culture Allows Rape to Go Unpunished

Jessica Bauer

Jessica Bauer writes a blog about current events and raising her two daughters in today's world.

Although the counseling centers on many college and university campuses see numerous rape victims, the school administrators respond minimally. Often the victims are ridiculed while the perpetrators go unpunished. As an example, in 2006 some members of the men's lacrosse team at North Carolina's Duke University were accused of raping a professional stripper. In this case, the university president did respond by suspending the accused students; however, the college community was outraged at the suspensions and defamed the victim. Young men need to learn respect for women and that violence is unacceptable; unfortunately, colleges and universities are promoting just the opposite.

I graduated from the University of Pittsburgh. During my sophomore year, I became a P.E.E.R. Educator (Peer Educators for an Environment free of Rape and Sexual Exploitation) through Sexual Assault Services which is housed in the counseling center. I also worked in the Sexual Assault Services office as a coordinator of the P.E.E.R. educators in my junior and senior years. P.E.E.R.'s presented materials designed at educating students about sexual assault. We did our presentations for the football team (nightmare), fraternities, sororities, freshman classes, etc. Once, I even taught a month long "semi-

Jessica Bauer, "Duke Rape Case Hits Raw Nerve," ReadingEagle.com, April 22, 2006. Reproduced by permission.

nar" on sexual harassment for three badly behaved boys who went around freshman dorms ripping open shower curtains of unsuspecting female students and snapping pictures. Nice. I loved what I did there and felt like I was really helping students. What I could never understand though, was why our counseling offices were full of appointments with former rape victims, yet our campus security stats were always wonderful. It didn't jive and I imagine that many universities have such a dirty little secret.

Victims Are Discounted

While I was a student at Pitt, there was a gang rape at a fraternity party. The girl was a freshman and it was early in the first semester. The rape happened in a bathroom and the girl was devastated. She had had too much to drink, no friends who watched out for her, and one thing led to another. The case rocked the university paper and that's all anyone really talked about. The fraternity was a large one and had at least 60 members at the time. Every single one of those guys knew who did what, yet each one of them kept their solemn brotherly vow and not a one would speak up and make right what a handful of them had done. The university did nothing. They didn't revoke their charter or suspend them from school. They only disallowed them from accepting pledges during the spring semester. Big freaking deal. The freshman student tried to stick it out at the school, but she was too much of a wreck and eventually quit college altogether. The counselor I worked for at Sexual Assault Services had tried to counsel and help her, but she was a broken woman. She had the guts to come forward, a freshman against an entire well known fraternity, and she was rewarded with nothing but harassment and disbelief. I often wonder about those boys and whether or not they can sleep at night. I wonder about whether or not they are now married with children, daughters perhaps. I wonder about how they must feel about what they did to that poor woman, whether they were part of the rape or part of the zipped lips.

The Duke Rape Case

Because of this, the Duke rape case [members of the men's lacrosse team were accused of rape in 2006] is driving me absolutely insane. You have a well known school, a sports team mentality, and a stripper's word against a band of "brothers." These are the things that are annoying me:

1. Just because she was intoxicated doesn't mean a rape did not occur. Most sexual assaults occur when the victim, the assailant(s) or both are intoxicated. This does not make her any less credible.

2. DNA evidence is not required to show that a rape occurred. (Please don't even make me explain the "anatomy" of this one.)

3. The fact that the second stripper says it happened or that it didn't happen, or that she believes it could have or could not have happened MEANS NOTHING. She was not in the bathroom. She does not know. The fact that she thinks it may or may not have happened is NOT evidence.

4. Why would the alleged victim make this up? What does she have to gain? The Duke lacrosse team and/or its members are not celebrities. There is absolutely NO upside to reporting a rape. Rape shield laws are complete crap these days. No one adheres to them in court. Reporting a rape of this magnitude makes you nothing more than a target. This is why the vast majority of rapes are not reported. Rape victims are forced to relive what's happened to them over and over and over and over again.

5. This has NOTHING to do with race. This is about a woman who was violated. It does not matter what color she is, or what color her attackers are. It's wrong any way you slice it.

6. Strippers are not "asking for it." Would I be a stripper? Never. I'd rather live out of a cardboard box and eat scraps on a street before I would take off my clothing for cash. But, some women strip for money. It does not mean they are asking to be raped. It seems to me, they're trying to make a living and there are a lot of men out there who are more than happy to pay for it.

I feel it's only appropriate for me to add here that the only thing worse than a group of guys sticking together and not saying a word about what they've done, is a "victim" who makes up the crime. As Jim Hines states in his article ["False Accusations"]:

> It happens. It's a legitimate fear. But it's not one I've got a lot of sympathy for. Not compared to the people who lived every night in fear that their father, mother, or some other relative would come in and molest them. Not compared to the women who struggled through fear, violation, and helplessness after a boy they trusted turned out to be a rapist. Not compared to the vast number of men and women who did speak out about their victimization, only to be labeled liars and sluts.

I wish I was bringing my girls up in a world where I didn't have to worry about what will happen to them when they're in college.

Few Encouraging Signs

The things that are encouraging about this case are that the students involved have been suspended, the coach is gone, and the University President actually had the guts to disallow them from playing any more games this year until this situation is resolved. For that, I am happy. Duke did more than a lot of schools do when faced with a similar situation.

I am dreading the outcome though, as I watch this case being played out in the media: lawyers dropping bits of information designed to prejudice a potential jury, lacrosse players and their parents lawyering up and zipping their lips, fellow strippers coming out to catch their 15 minutes of fame no matter what damage they may be doing to themselves, their friend, or women in general. It all makes me sick. I wish I was bringing my girls up in a world where I didn't have to worry about what will happen to them when they're in college, where they didn't have to view every man as a potential problem before finally being able to trust him, where I could be sure that young men are being brought up right, to respect and cherish the women who will be in their lives. But unfortunately, it's just not that way and giving birth to daughters, for me, means a lifetime of worrying.

11

Legislation Is Needed to Protect Rape Victims

Emily Charlap

Emily Charlap is an intern with the National Organization for Women and attended the congressional briefing in 2005 hosted by Girls Inc.

A growing number of young women are at risk of being sexually assaulted. Often these assaults are waved off as being the victim's fault, leaving the young woman with no physical or emotional care. The Violence Against Women Act (VAWA) 2005 would expand direct services such as shelters, counseling, and legal help to encompass young victims. It would also provide funding to expand prevention and education programs regarding gender-based violence for both girls and boys. Because it includes minors, the VAWA 2005 is vital in breaking the cycle of violence.

Editor's Note: President George W. Bush signed the VAWA 2005 into law on January 5, 2006.

The landmark Violence Against Women Act (VAWA) of 1994 must be reauthorized this year [2005], and VAWA supporters expect the bill to include language that addresses violence against young people. Our nation cannot say it addresses violence unless we make sure there is VAWA funding for youth violence prevention and treatment.

At a Congressional briefing hosted by Girls Inc. May 11 [2005], advocates, professionals and young women affected by

Emily Charlap, "VAWA 2005 Could Curb Violence in Girls' Lives," National Organization for Women.org, May 13, 2005. Reproduced by permission.

violence and abuse talked about the growing problem of gender-based violence—from sexual assault and date rape to family violence and stalking. The audience heard over and over how VAWA 2005 could be an even greater force than before in addressing the overall problem of violence against young women and girls. The proposed bill includes education to break the cycle of violence, as well as enhanced funding for treatment and direct services to young survivors.

Young Women Need Protection

Young women suffer the greatest risk of rape and sexual assault. A young woman can experience this violence in many places: in her home, her school, her relationships and her community. Sadly, young women who are raped or sexually assaulted almost always know the perpetrator.

Nearly one in three high-school-age women experience some type of abuse—whether physical, sexual or psychological—in their dating relationships. During the 1999–2000 school year, the U.S. Department of Education reported 628 rapes or attempted rapes, 4,261 cases of sexual battery other than rape and 127,568 incidents of sexual harassment on public school grounds. Yet, public school systems rarely report such incidents. This kind of abuse of young women, perpetrated by both young men and other young women is seen by some adults as normal, or at least avoidable. Such incidents are waved off with: "she shouldn't have worn that," or "she shouldn't have acted that way"—the game we're all familiar with, Blame the Victim.

Shannon Eaves, a member of the Girls Inc. Girls Advisory Board, and a freshman at San Francisco State University, shared a personal story with the group gathered at the May 11 [2005] briefing. A friend of Eaves was raped repeatedly by a trusted adult in her community. When the victim mustered up the courage to speak out about the attack—despite her attacker's threats—community members called her a liar. Not only did the community turn their backs on the girl, but her family chose to neither support nor believe her. To add insult to injury, she had no place to go because of a complete lack of confidential shelters and rape crisis centers in her area.

Eaves and others pooled resources to put their friend up in a motel for a few days, and then took her to stay at her grandmother's house, where she was helped in rebuilding the relationship with the rest of her family. Though the girl is back at home and even attending community college, there are still emotional consequences of both the attack and the lack of support and direct services that followed. Such an incident is not isolated, not even in this young victim's own life.

Young People Need Education and Support

This story is just one of millions that could be told by millions of women across the nation. Girls need help and VAWA 2005 is being drafted to provide that help.

It's terrible enough that women and girls suffer sexual assault, rape and domestic abuse. But should they also be left to deal with it on their own? We need to expand the direct services like shelters, counseling and legal help that were put in place by the original VAWA and continue to raise awareness that these services exist. VAWA 2005 can address these needs by adding more funding for such services, including more funding for culturally specific services in communities where that type of specialized services can be most effective.

Zanae Cook, a 14-year-old eighth-grader from Philadelphia, also shared her story at the briefing May 11 [2005]. Cook suffered harassment from another young woman on a public bus while her friends and strangers watched in silence. Instead of combating violence with violence, Cook remained calm while being spit on and verbally harassed. In a Girls Inc. after-school program, she learned to recognize various types of violence, as well as different methods to break the cycle of violence.

More young women and girls need to learn how to recognize and respond to violence. Fortunately such programs already exist and with adequate funding the programs could be expanded to educate more and more young people—both girls and boys. Young men and boys need to be educated about the role they can play in stopping gender-based violence. Adult men also need to be reminded that they are role models for the younger generations, and can affect boys' behavior. Men and boys need to understand that violence against women and girls is unacceptable in all of society. By including minors in VAWA 2005, these vital education and prevention programs can be funded and we can break the cycle of violence.

12

Legislation Is Not Needed to Protect Rape Victims

Wendy McElroy

Wendy McElroy is the editor of ifeminists.com and the author of Sexual Correctness: The Gender Feminist Attack on Women.

The first Violence Against Women Act (VAWA) was passed in 1994 and arose because domestic violence had become a serious social problem that needed attention. However, the VAWA focused the issue on women victims to the exclusion of men and male children. Despite the protest by men's rights activists, the VAWA was reauthorized in 2000 and was given increased funding of $3.3 billion. Research indicates that traditionally defined violence against women has declined, yet VAWA 2005 seeks even more funding; some anti-VAWA objections suggest the money is needed for political purposes rather than for victims' aid. Congress should not reauthorize the VAWA, not only because it discriminates against males, but also because of the unaccountability and misuse of its funding.

Editor's Note: President George W. Bush signed the VAWA 2005 into law on January 5, 2006.

The Violence Against Women Act (VAWA) will expire this September [2005] if it is not reauthorized by Congress. Largely viewed as an anti-domestic violence measure, VAWA has become a flashpoint for the men's rights advocates who see it instead as the living symbol of anti-male bias in law.

Wendy McElroy, "Congress Should Kill Discriminatory Domestic Violence Act," ifeminists.com, June 29, 2005.

VAWA Ignores Male Victims

Although a significant number of domestic violence victims are male, VAWA defines victims as female. As one result, tax-funded domestic violence shelters and services assist women and routinely turn away men, often including older male children.

Estimates vary on the prevalence of male victims. Professor Martin Fiebert of California State University at Long Beach offers a bibliography that "summarizes 170 scholarly investigations, 134 empirical studies and 36 reviews."

It indicates that men and women are victimized at much the same rate. A lower-bound figure is provided by a recent DOJ [Department of Justice] study: Men constituted 27 percent of the victims of family violence between 1998 and 2002.

Accordingly, men's rights activists not only accuse the VAWA of not merely being unconstitutional for excluding men but also of dismissing the existence of one-quarter to one-half of domestic violence victims.

VAWA Creates a Distorted Picture

The criticism should go deeper. In many ways, VAWA typifies the legislative approach to social problems, which arose over the past few decades and peaked during the Clinton years.

The legislative approach follows a pattern: public furor stirs over a social problem; Congress is pressured to "do something"; remedial bureaucracy arises, often with scant planning; the problem remains; more money and bureaucracy is demanded; those who object are called hostile to "victims."

VAWA arose largely from the concern stirred by feminists in the '80s. They quite properly focused on domestic violence as a neglected and misunderstood social problem. But their analysis went to extremes and seemed tailor-made to create public furor.

As an example, consider a widely circulated claim: "a woman is beaten every 15 seconds." The statistic is sometimes attributed to the FBI, other times to a 1983 report by the Department of Justice's Bureau of Justice Statistics. But neither the FBI nor the DOJ sites seems to include that statement or a similar one.

Men's rights activists contend that the elusive statistic derives from the book *"Behind Closed Doors: Violence in the American Family"* (1980) by Murray Straus, Richard J. Gelles and Suzanne K. Steinmetz. The book was based on the first National Family Violence Survey (1975), from which the FBI and other federal agencies drew.

The survey does support the claim that a woman is battered every 15 seconds but also indicates men are also victims. By omitting male victims from their efforts, however, domestic violence activists create the impression of a national epidemic that uniquely victimizes women who require unique protection.

In response to public outcry, Congress was pressured to "do something." It passed VAWA 1994, granting $1.6 billion to create a bureaucracy of researchers, advocates, experts, and victim assistants, which some collectively call "the domestic violence industry."

Data indicates that traditionally defined violence against women has declined sharply.

Reauthorized in 2000, VAWA's funding rose to $3.33 billion to be expended over five years. Now, VAWA 2005 seeks more money.

VAWA Wants More Money

Voices like the National Organization for Women [NOW] insist that "the problem" remains. To argue for the "growing problem of gender-based violence," however, NOW reaches beyond traditionally defined violence against women and seeks to protect high school girls from abusive dating experiences.

NOW states, "Nearly one in three high-school-age women experience some type of abuse—whether physical, sexual or psychological—in their dating relationships."

Without expanding the definition in such a manner, it would be difficult to argue for more funding.

Data indicates that traditionally defined violence against women has declined sharply. The rate of family violence reportedly "fell from about 5.4 victims per 1,000 to 2.1 victims per 1,000 people 12 and older," according to DOJ statistics.

VAWA 2005 faces much more opposition than its earlier incarnations. One reason is that men's rights activists have been presenting counter-data and arguments for over 10 years.

Objections point to those dollars being used for political purposes rather than clear and immediate assistance to victims.

Advocates of VAWA 2005 have responded with pre-emptive accusations that paint opponents as anti-victim: for example, "If Congress does not act quickly to reauthorize the legislation, they are putting women's and children's lives at risk."

But most of the anti-VAWA arguments are not anti-victim. Many are anti-bureaucracy and could apply to any of the so-called "industries" created by the legislative approach to social problems. (The Child Protective Services is another example.)

Some anti-bureaucracy objections focus on the billions of dollars transferred into programs, often with little oversight or accountability attached.

Other objections point to those dollars being used for political purposes rather than clear and immediate assistance to victims. The misuse of tax dollars is most often alleged on the grassroots level, where men's rights activists often face VAWA-funded opposition to political measures, especially on father's rights issues.

One incident in New Hampshire illustrates the point. Earlier this year [2005], The Presumption of Shared Parental Rights and Responsibilities Act was defeated by vehement opposition from the New Hampshire Coalition Against Domestic and Sexual Violence. The coalition both wrote to and spoke before the Legislature. Accordingly, father's rights advocates in New Hampshire are seeking language in VAWA 2005 to prohibit any VAWA-funded agency from "legislative lobbying, advertising, or otherwise supporting the endorsement of, or opposition to, any state proposed legislation" which is not explicitly related to the prevention of domestic violence.

I think they should seek to kill the act entirely. I believe VAWA is not only ideologically inspired and discriminatory, it is also an example of why bureaucracy-driven solutions to human problems do not work.

I hope VAWA becomes the Titanic of the legislative approach to social problems. I hope it sinks spectacularly.

13

People Who Make False Rape Accusations Should Be Severely Punished

Jonna M. Spilbor

Jonna M. Spilbor, a criminal defense attorney, has covered many of the nation's high-profile criminal trials as a guest commentator on Court TV and other television news networks.

Although there are no accurate statistics on the number of false rape claims, the fact remains that false rape claims are indeed made—usually to cover up a sexual affair or to retaliate against the accused for a past slight. Regardless of the motive behind them, such false accusations not only devastate the lives of the accused, but also demean the many true rape victims who deserve justice. Currently accusers who lie receive insignificant consequences; therefore, in order to deter people from crying rape when none occurred, states should make the crime of false reporting a felony with serious penalties imposed. In addition, states should allow juries to deliver an official finding that the accuser lied.

Last Wednesday, August 6 [2003], in what amounted to a highly publicized yet rare spectacle, Kobe Bryant was arraigned on a felony sex assault charge. There was no familiar gold jersey, no basket, and no opposing team to speak of, but that didn't stop the crowd outside the Eagle County [Colorado] Courthouse from rooting wildly for Bryant.

Jonna M. Spilbor, "What If Kobe Bryant Has Been Falsely Accused? Why the Law of Acquaintance and Date Rape Should Seriously Penalize False Reports," Findlaw.com, August 11, 2003. Reproduced by permission.

Bryant arrived at the courthouse via private jet, stayed for eight minutes, and uttered but two words: "No, Sir." Bryant's beautiful young wife, Vanessa, and her equally stunning, four million dollar, get-out-of-the-doghouse diamond ring did not accompany him to the event. But his diminutive attorney, Pamela Mackey, and her partner, Hal Haddon, did—with Mackey doing all the talking.

Bryant's next scheduled court appearance, a preliminary hearing, has been set for October 9—just two days after he will have played his first preseason game of the 2003/2004 basketball season.

Meanwhile, it's become clear that the prosecutors are going after Bryant with a vengeance. Eagle County District Attorney Mark Hurlbert asked for an additional $105,000 from the state budget to cover anticipated expenses in this matter. The budget Commissioner not only granted his wish, but went further, allotting him $150,000 dollars, nearly a third more than requested, so he would have a "buffer."

Bryant's case has raised a firestorm of issues, but one in particular is at center court: Has this good guy been falsely accused? Even at this early stage, the majority of those asked say yes. To many fans, this case just *feels* false.

If Bryant has been falsely accused, it won't be the first time that a false report has been filed in an "acquaintance rape" case. In part, that's because the law fails to meaningfully penalize false reports, or to give those who have been falsely accused any justice.

False Rape Reports Are Especially Harmful

The statistics on false rape reports in the U.S. are widely divergent, and often too outdated to be meaningful. Not surprisingly, the numbers also depend on whom you ask. Organizations that tout a feminist agenda claim the number of false rape reports to be nearly non-existent—about two percent. But other organizations, taking the side of men, claim that false reports are actually very common—citing numbers ranging from forty-one to sixty percent.

Amid the statistics, the truth is impossible to ascertain—but it's plain that false reports are indeed made, and that they can ruin the life of the accused, whether or not a conviction follows.

Falsely reporting any crime is shameful. Falsely reporting a rape is especially heinous. The liar who files the false claim dishonors—and makes life all the more difficult for—the many true victims who file genuine rape claims because they have been terribly violated, and seek justice for it. At the same time, and perhaps even more seriously, the false report begins to destroy the reputation, and sometimes the life, of the accused from the very moment it is made—a fact of which many accusers are keenly aware.

This phenomenon of "conviction before trial" is especially acute in Bryant's case. One of his current sponsors, Nutella, has already pulled out because of the present allegations. Will Nutella re-sign him to an endorsement contract if he is ultimately acquitted? It's doubtful—and in any case, Bryant's pride may counsel him not to accept.

There Are Two Basic Types of False Allegations

In my experience as a criminal defense attorney, I've found that false "acquaintance rape" and "date rape" accusers tend to fall into two rough categories.

First, there are those who seek revenge against the accused: the jilted lover, disgruntled employee, or custody-seeking ex. Their reason for wanting to cause harm to the accused is transparent. Fortunately, that usually means it is also easily exposed to both judge and jury.

Second, there are those who seek not to annihilate another's reputation, but instead to preserve their own—albeit at another's expense. Some are young women who are trying to cover up, to their parents, the fact that they are already sexually active. Others are men or women in relationships who are trying to cover up, to their partners, that they have committed an infidelity.

A seemingly remorseful witness once told me, "I knew if I cheated, my boyfriend would beat me. The only way out of the beating, for me, was to play the rape card." You read it correctly: The rape card.

Not too long ago, I represented an Ivy League honor student who'd spent a weekend at a beach party coupled with a woman to whom he was introduced by a mutual friend. According to the client—and about a dozen witnesses—the two seemed to really "hit it off." When the party ended on Sunday night, they said their good-byes, like everybody else, and maybe even promised half-heartedly to call each other.

States should make the crime of false reporting a felony, with penalties serious enough to have a strong deterrent effect.

Imagine my client's surprise when on Tuesday, he received an angry call from his paramour's estranged boyfriend—a boyfriend whose existence she failed to disclose when the pair were kissing beyond the crackle of a bonfire.

Of course, this was nothing compared to his total shock when, two weeks later, he received a warrant in the mail commanding his appearance in court on felony rape charges.

False Rape Accusations Should Have Serious Penalties

There are several ways in which states may crack down on false rape reports, while still allowing genuine rape claims to be successfully prosecuted.

First, states can increase penalties for false reporting, which are often minimal.

For instance, in Colorado—where Kobe Bryant will be tried—the crime of "False Reporting to Authorities"—"mak-[ing] a report . . . to law enforcement authorities of a crime or other incident when [the reporter] knows that it did not occur"—is merely a class three misdemeanor.

Accordingly, the maximum penalty for a violation is a fine, ranging from fifty-bucks to $750, and up to six months in the county jail. And of course, someone without a prior criminal record is highly unlikely to serve more than a few weeks, if any time at all. Meanwhile, a misdemeanor conviction is not the kind of blemish on one's record that will likely stop a false accuser from getting a job, enrolling in college, or even voting for president.

States should make the crime of false reporting a felony, with penalties serious enough to have a strong deterrent effect. Currently, the stakes are far too low for the accuser, given how very high they are for the accused.

Compare Bryant's exposure: If found guilty, he will serve a sentence up to life in prison. He would also be branded a Class A felon, and most likely, a sex offender. (Even when released, he'd face slim prospects: He was drafted into the NBA at the tender age of 17, and thus lacks the college education upon which many other professional athletes can fall back on.)

In sum, he will move from stardom and security to incarceration and, later, Megan's List. Shouldn't an accuser who has forced him to risk this fate, also risk consequences herself if she is lying?

Juries Should Officially Designate That An Accuser Lied

In addition to imposing serious penalties for false reports, states should also give juries that conclude the accuser has lied, a way to voice that finding—allowing them to render a "Not Credible" verdict along with their "Not Guilty" verdict. Otherwise, the taint of the prosecution will linger.

An acquittal, of course, only means the prosecution has failed to prove its case beyond a reasonable doubt—and the public knows it. So to truly get justice, one who is falsely accused needs more than an acquittal: He needs a finding that the accuser lied.

The current law, however, simply ignores that the false report has happened. It's not just that it doesn't provide for a "Not Credible" verdict. It's also that it gives a false accuser a second bite at the apple: She (or he) can still go on to bring a civil case for damages. Because the standard of proof in a civil suit is lower, it is not precluded by an acquittal.

Perhaps a "Not Credible" verdict, then, ought to bar a future civil suit by the accuser, as well. It only makes sense: A finding of a lie ought to prevent the false accuser from using that lie as the basis for a future case.

The Current Justice System Fails the Falsely Accused

One might point out that the falsely accused do have some recourse, even in the current system: They, too, can avail themselves of the criminal and civil justice systems, at least in theory. But in reality, these remedies too often miss the mark.

Are the prosecutors who indicted Bryant really going to do an about-face, after an acquittal, to go after his accuser? The chances of that happening are about as great as Kobe's wife trading in that four-million-dollar rock for a shopping spree at K-Mart.

And even if the prosecutors did so, they'd lose before the jury, precisely because of that about-face: Jurors would doubtless think, "You believed in her credibility enough to try to send Bryant to jail—now suddenly you believe she's a liar? I don't buy it, at least not enough to give you a 'beyond a reasonable doubt' conviction."

What about civil suits? To begin, forget about suing the prosecutor's office: Governmental immunity will most likely shield it from liability.

And while a civil suit by the accused against the accuser would be possible, it's not likely either. Defamation law includes a "judicial proceedings privilege" that makes it hard to sue based on testimony.

Accusers have little to fear under current law if they lie.

Meanwhile, contingency-fee attorneys may be disinclined to accept as a client someone who so recently was thought to be a criminal—and presented as one in the public eye. Their bread-and-butter is their ability to choose cases that are likely winners; an ex-defendant's case may not seem to be one of them.

Finally, the accused may, quite understandably, simply prefer to put this terrible chapter of his life behind him. And he may fear losing his civil suit, even if he's telling the absolute truth—in the end, it will still be essentially a "he said, she said" case.

For all these reasons, most of those who are falsely accused cannot get any kind of justice, either civil or criminal. And Kobe Bryant, if he has been falsely accused, will be no different.

Penalties Are Needed to Prevent False Rape Reports

Society rightly makes great efforts to protect victims (who are usually women) against the ravages of rape and sexual assault. But shouldn't we also do more to better protect defendants (virtually always men) from being wrongfully accused?

False reports of rape are like other crimes: They can be deterred. Such reports are easy to make—all they require is a phone call and a police interview. They are also devastating.

Yet accusers have little to fear, under current law, if they lie. If the stakes were higher, then those holding the "rape card" might see fit to fold.

Kobe Bryant's accuser may be telling the truth. If so, terrible consequences may follow for him. Or, she may be lying. If so, the consequences for her will likely be slight. That asymmetry needs to be remedied—and the law needs to take false reports of rape seriously, just as it takes rape itself seriously. Both can be life-destroying for the victim; both should be punished appropriately by our legal system.

14

Finding Justice in Rape Cases Is Difficult

Dahlia Lithwick

Dahlia Lithwick, a graduate of Yale University and Stanford Law School, is a Slate *senior editor and writes "Supreme Court Dispatches."*

Sometimes rape cases are reduced to he said/she said claims, and it becomes a spin of the roulette wheel to decide whom to believe. With cases in which physical evidence exists, it is possible to skew the evidence one way or another depending on how it is presented. Accusers, defendants, lawyers, jurors, onlookers all have preconceived notions about an event based on their own deep-seated belief systems and personal experiences. Taking all of those factors into account, finding clear and objective truths in rape cases is almost, but not completely, insurmountable.

Here we go again.

The Duke lacrosse team's rape scandal [in 2006] cuts too deeply into this country's most tender places: race and class and gender. It reaffirms everyone's deep-seated, unspoken fear that black women/white men/poor people/privileged people/ victims/defendants can't get a fair shake under our legal system. This case will be chewed over, regurgitated, and chewed over again by television pundits unafraid of venturing opinions in no way informed or changed by the rapidly changing public facts.

Dahlia Lithwick, "Lacrosse Purposes: How We Fool Ourselves into Believing We Are Dispassionate About the Duke Case," Slate.com, April 22, 2006. Reproduced by permission.

It's easy to have doubts about the ability of the courts to resolve cases like this one when you stop to consider that long after the court proceedings, hearings, and investigations ended, we still have no idea what really happened between Kobe Bryant [professional basketball player accused of rape] and his accuser, between Michael Jackson [singer accused of child molestation] and his accuser, between Clarence Thomas [Supreme Court justice] and Anita Hill [law professor who claimed sexual harassment]. If these legal processes are intended to be searches for the truth, why is there never any truth at the conclusion?

Some Truths Are Elusive

Part of the answer is that some truths are unknowable. Subtle distinctions between consensual sex and date rape, between coercion and force, between silences that sound like "yes" and silences that sound like "stop," are difficult for the parties themselves to work out. How can a juror really divine what went on in the mind of another person?

But that's where the Duke case truly differs from the Kobe Bryant case. This is not a case about consent. Either a forcible rape, kidnapping, and strangulation happened in that bathroom in Durham or it didn't. This wasn't a date gone wrong. At the margins, this case may be about sex and race and power. But it's not about subtle social messages or identity-based misunderstandings. It's about an assault.

Also, there is evidence here: Mounds and mounds of significant physical evidence. There is a rape kit. There are bruises, and then, apparently, more bruises. There are DNA tests and broken fingernails and witnesses seemingly tumbling out of the woodwork. There are time-stamped photographic accounts of much of the evening. This is not a classic "he says/she says." The evidence has something to say to us as well.

Perhaps we should be thankful that this is not a case about ESP as much as it's a case about CSI [Crime Scene Investigation].

Some Truths Are Subjective

One might hope that all this evidence, and the unambiguous legal charges, would lead to reasonable legal inferences and unequivocal legal conclusions. But that is where we'd be dead wrong. Because the so-called objective "evidence" currently being meticulously weighed and evaluated by the media is no more "objective" or "conclusive" than the rank speculation by the pundits. Everything we are hearing about the DNA tests and the photos is selective, secondhand, and anecdotal. We are being played by the lawyers, with leaks and well-chosen sound bites.

We look to the facts to confirm our own pre-existing suspicions.

The same thing happened after the Kobe Bryant accusations surfaced. People made instant judgments—based on their own experiences, or what they read in the paper, and what they knew to be true in their bones. People thousands of miles from that resort in Colorado knew for certain that Bryant's accuser was a liar and a tramp. Women who had never even heard of Kobe Bryant knew absolutely that he was a rapist.

And that's what's happening in the Duke case. We already feel we know, with great certainty, who's lying and who isn't. The headmaster of one of the accused students' old high school puts out a statement saying: "Knowing Reade Seligmann as well as we do here at Delbarton . . . I believe him innocent of the charges included in the indictment." A Duke English professor has called for the university to expel the whole lacrosse team to stop the "drunken white male privilege loosed amongst us."

Rush Limbaugh [radio talk show host], knowing nothing about these people, comfortably dismisses the alleged victim as a "ho." (I gather he apologized. Huzzah.) Jesse Jackson [civil rights activist], knowing nothing about this nameless accuser, is comfortable saying this is an archetypal racial conflict:

> Black women; white men. A stripper; and a team blowout. The wealthy white athletes—many from prep schools—of Duke; and the working class woman from historically black North Carolina Central. Race and class and sex. What happened? We don't know for sure because the Duke players are maintaining a code of silence. The history of white men and black women—the special fantasies and realities of exploitation—goes back to the nation's beginning and the arrival of slaves from Africa.

And Tucker Carlson [television news show host] doesn't hesitate to impugn the truthfulness of anyone employed as a "crypto-hooker."

Such comments—about total strangers, involving facts that are still largely unknown—tell us absolutely nothing. Or, if they tell us anything at all, it's about what happens in the creepy closet under the stairs of Limbaugh's, Jackson's, and Carlson's brains.

As was the case with O.J. Simpson [accused wife murderer found not guilty], Bryant, and Jackson, this is very quickly becoming an ink-blot test, not a legal proceeding: We look to the facts to confirm our own pre-existing suspicions about what inevitably happens between men and women, rich people and poor people, black people and white people.

Evidence Can Be Contradictory

And what about all this "physical evidence?" That unambiguous, objective scientific evidence? Supporters of the Duke students say the lack of a DNA match exonerates them. Peter Neufeld of the Innocence Project says, "There's an old saying that the absence of evidence is not necessarily evidence of absence." Nurses say the injuries are consistent with rape. The boys say someone else raped her. Time-stamped photos suggest the alleged victim was already injured before she arrived at the party. Other time-stamped photos suggest new injuries occurred while she was there. Lost fake fingernails in the bathroom suggest a fight. The lack of any DNA material under those nails suggest she never fought back. Photos say she was intoxicated upon arrival. The second stripper implies she was drugged at the party.

Pick your fact, any fact. Each of them can, it seems, be spun both ways. This scandal has become yet another exercise in fiction-writing as opposed to truth-seeking; we can use the same evidence to confirm what we already know in our bones to be true.

This case serves as yet another depressing reminder of all that is wrong with this country: Our sons are spoiled misogynistic bigots, and our colleges are hotbeds of polarizing identity politics. Race and gender and poverty still tear us apart. But this case may also serve as a sober reminder that courts are not laboratories and jurors are not scientists. Facts are, more often than not, just our own subjective opinions, dressed up to look like incontrovertible truths. There are, in the end, objective truths to be found here. But the jurors must work hard to look past their prejudices, and the lawyers' spin, to find them.

Organizations to Contact

Campus Outreach Services, Inc. (COS)
(610) 989-0651 • fax: (610) 989-0652
e-mail: info@campusoutreachservices.com
Web site: www.campusoutreachservices.com

COS is a for-profit organization that conducts date-rape prevention programs at colleges and high schools across the country. The company was founded by date-rape survivor and activist Katie Koestner to educate young people about the harm that date rape continues to cause women. The COS Web site provides free access to articles discussing the effectiveness of antirape programs and policies.

Center for Women Policy Studies (CWPS)
1776 Massachusetts Avenue NW, Suite 450
Washington, DC 20036
(202) 872-1770 • fax: (202) 296-8962
e-mail: cwps@centerwomenpolicy.org
Web site: www.centerwomenpolicy.org

The CWPS is an independent feminist policy research and advocacy institution established in 1972. The center studies policies affecting the social, legal, health, and economic status of women. It publishes numerous reports on violence against women, including *Victims No More: Girls Fight Back Against Male Violence* and *Does It Have to Be Like This?: Teen Women Ask Their Peers About Violence, Hate, and Discrimination*.

FaithTrust Institute
2400 N. 45th Street, Suite 10, Seattle, WA 98103
(206) 634-1903 • fax: (206) 634-0115
e-mail: info@faithtrustinstitute.org
Web site: http://faithtrustinstitute.org

Formally the Center for the Prevention of Sexual and Domestic Violence, the FaithTrust Institute is an international multifaith education resource center that works to end sexual and domestic violence. The institute offers training, consultation, and educational materials. Its publications include the quarterly newsletter *Working Together* and the books *Sexual Violence: The Sin Revisited and Men's Work in Preventing Violence Against Women.*

Hope for Healing
153 E. Broadway Blvd., #113, Jefferson City, TN   37760
e-mail: gayle@hopeforhealing.org
Web site: www.hopeforhealing.org

Hope for Healing is a source of information and support on the Internet for survivors of sexual and domestic violence. The organization publishes the *Healing News* newsletter that is written by and for rape survivors about rape recovery. It also offers links for help regarding teen dating violence.

Ifeminists
e-mail: info@ifeminists.net
Web site: www.ifeminists.net

Ifeminists, or individual feminists, is an online forum for women who believe that more women should accept personal responsibility for their decisions. The group respects viewpoints that do not always agree with the orthodoxy of politically correct feminism, and it dismisses the notion that the government knows what is best for women. Ifeminists publishes weekly editorials and numerous articles on its Web site that are skeptical of feminist research on date rape, sexual abuse, and other issues affecting women.

Independent Women's Forum (IWF)
1726 M Street NW, 10th Floor, Washington, DC   20036
(202) 419-1820
e-mail: info@iwf.org
Web site: www.iwf.org

The IWF advocates the conservative values of personal responsibility and self-reliance among women. It presents commentary opposed to the feminist movement's influence on the legal, economic, and educational spheres of American society. The forum publishes the *Women's Quarterly*, the monthly *Ex Femina* newsletter, and *She Thinks: Outrage of the Month*, a monthly magazine critical of the feminist movement on college campuses.

Men Can Stop Rape

PO Box 57144, Washington, DC   20037
(202) 265-6530 • fax: (202) 265-4362
e-mail: info@mencanstoprape.org
Web site: www.mencanstoprape.org

Men Can Stop Rape advocates male youth to work with women in preventing rape and other forms of men's violence. Through workshops and training programs, the organization promotes peace, equity, and gender justice. Among its publications are the weekly e-newsletter "Safe & Strong," and the information sheets, "Why Rape Is a Men's Issue," "What Men Can Do," and "Male Survivors."

Ms. Foundation for Women

120 Wall Street, 33rd Floor, New York, NY   10005
(212) 742-2300 • fax: (212) 742-1653
e-mail: info@ms.foundation.org
Web site: www.ms.foundation.org

The foundation provided the funding for Mary Koss's widely cited 1985 study on the high incidence of date rape on college campuses, and it continues to conduct training and public education programs to protect the safety and health of women. The foundation's publications include the quarterly *Ms. Foundation* newsletter and numerous reports and pamphlets, including *Stopping the Violence Against Women: The Movement from Intervention to Prevention* and *Safety & Justice For All: Examining the Relationship Between the Women's Anti-Violence Movement and the Criminal Legal System.*

**National Association of College and
University Attorneys (NACUA)**
One Dupont Circle, Suite 620, Washington, DC 20036
(202) 833-8390 • fax: (202) 296-8379
e-mail: nacua@nacua.org
Web site: www.nacua.org

The association is comprised of nearly fifteen hundred U.S.
and Canadian colleges represented by over thirty-four hundred attorneys. It compiles and distributes legal decisions,
opinions, and other writings and information on legal problems affecting colleges and universities. Publications include
Crime on Campus and *Sexual Harassment on Campus: A Legal
Compendium.*

National Center for Victims of Crime (NCVC)
2000 M Street NW, Suite 480, Washington, DC 20036
(202) 467-8700 • fax: (202) 467-8701
e-mail: webmaster@ncvc.org
Web site: www.ncvc.org

The National Center for Victims of Crime is a resource and
advocacy organization for crime victims. It provides direct
services and resources, advocates for passage of laws and public policies that secure rights and protections for crime victims, and delivers training and technical assistance to victim
service organizations and counselors. Its publications include
the report "Our Vulnerable Teenagers: Their Victimization, Its
Consequences, and Directions for Prevention and Intervention," and the study "Rape in America: A Report to the Nation."

National Center on Addiction and Substance Abuse (CASA)
Columbia University, New York, NY 10017-6706
(212) 841-5200
Web site: www.casacolumbia.org

CASA conducts research to understand and reduce the social
cost of substance abuse. It publishes several reports investigat-
ing how substance abuse can lead to sexual assaults, including

2004 CASA National Survey of American Attitudes on Substance Abuse IX: Teen Dating Practices and Sexual Activity and *Dangerous Liaisons: Substance Abuse and Sex.*

National Coalition of Free Men (NCFM)
PO Box 582023, Minneapolis, MN 55458-2023
(888) 223-1280
e-mail: ncfm@ncfm.org
Web site: www.ncfm.org

The coalition is a nonprofit education and civil rights organization that seeks "a fair and balanced perspective on gender issues." It promotes men's legal rights in matters such as false accusation of rape, sexual harassment, and sexual abuse. The coalition conducts research, sponsors educational programs, maintains a database on men's issues, and publishes the bimonthly newsletter *Transitions: Journal of Men's Perspectives.*

National Organization for Women (NOW)
1100 H Street NW, 3rd Floor, Washington, DC 20005
(202) 628-8669 • fax: (202) 785-8576
Web site: www.now.org

The National Organization for Women is the largest organization of feminist activists in the United States. It works to bring about equality for all women and eliminate discrimination, harassment, and all forms of violence against women. The organization educates the public and the media about the status of and threats to women's rights, initiates and supports lawsuits against violators of women's rights, and lobbies for laws that promote full equality for women. It offers a comprehensive list of publications including books, articles, reports, and briefs.

National Sexual Violence Resource Center (NSVRC)
123 N. Enola Drive, Enola, PA 17025
(877) 739-3895 • fax: (717) 909-0714
e-mail: resources@nsvrc.org
Web site: www.nsvrc.org

NSVRC is a comprehensive collection and distribution center for information, research, and emerging policy on sexual violence and prevention. The center provides an extensive online library and coordinates National Sexual Assault Awareness Month initiatives. It produces the *Resource Newsletter* twice yearly and numerous booklets, including "Sexual Violence and the Spectrum of Prevention: Towards a Community Solution" and "Unspoken Crimes: Sexual Assault in Rural America."

Office for Victims of Crime Resource Center
U.S. Department of Justice, Washington, DC   20531
(800) 851-3420
e-mail: askov@ojp.usdoj.gov
Web site: www.ojp.usdoj.gov/ovc

Established in 1983 by the U.S. Department of Justice's Office for Victims of Crime, the resource center is a primary source of information regarding victim-related issues. It answers questions using national and regional statistics, research findings, and a network of victim advocates and organizations. The center publishes numerous reports on sexual assault, including *Patterns of Violence Against Women: Risk Factors and Consequences.*

Rape, Abuse & Incest National Network (RAINN)
2000 L Street NW, Suite 406, Washington, DC   20036
(202) 544-1034 • fax: (202) 544-3556
e-mail: info@rainn.org
Web site: www.rainn.org

RAINN operates the National Sexual Assault hotline and provides information about sexual assault prevention, recovery, and prosecution. The network also works to improve services to victims and ensure that rapists are brought to justice.

Sex Infomation and Education Council of the U.S. (SIECUS)
130 W. 42nd Street, Suite 350, New York, NY   10036-7802
(202) 819-9770 • fax: (212) 819-9776

e-mail: siecus@siecus.org
Web site: www.siecus.org

SIECUS is a clearinghouse for information on sexuality, with a special interest in sex education. It publishes sex education curricula, the bimonthly newsletter *SIECUS Report*, and fact sheets on sex education issues. Its articles, bibliographies, and book reviews often address the role of sex education in identifying, reducing, and preventing sexual violence.

Wellesley Centers for Women (WCW)
Wellesley College, Wellesley, MA   02481
(781) 283-2500 • fax: (781) 283-2504
e-mail: wcw@wellesley.edu
Web site: www.wcwonline.org

The Wellesley Centers for Women is a liberal, pro-feminist community of scholars engaged in research and training efforts to improve the lives of women. It publishes the results of its numerous research projects and the *Research & Action Report*.

Bibliography

Books

Colleen Adams	*Rohypnol: Roofies—the Date-Rape Drug.* New York: Rosen, 2006.
Clint E. Bruess and Jerrold S. Greenberg	*Sexuality Education: Theory and Practice.* Sudbury, MA: Jones and Bartlett, 2004.
Faith Hickman Brynie	*101 Questions About Sex and Sexuality.* Brookfield, CT: Twenty-First Century, 2003.
Emilie Buchwald, Pamela Fletcher, Martha Roth (eds.)	*Transforming a Rape Culture.* Minneapolis: Milkweed Editions, 2005.
Janell L. Carroll and Paul Root Wolpe	*Sexuality Now: Embracing Diversity.* Belmont, CA: Thomson Wadsworth, 2005.
Mark Cowling and Paul Reynolds	*Making Sense of Sexual Consent.* Burlington, VT: Ashgate, 2004.
Robert Crooks and Karla Baur	*Our Sexuality.* Belmont, CA: Thomson Wadsworth, 2005.
Richard Doyle	*Family Issues.* Morrisville, NC: Lulu Press, 2006.

Patricia Easteal and Louise McOrmond-Plummer	*Real Rape, Real Pain: Help for Women Sexually Assaulted by Male Partners.* Victoria, Australia: Hybrid, 2006.
Paula Ruth Gilbert and Kimberly K. Eby	*Violence and Gender: An Interdisciplinary Reader.* Upper Saddle River, NJ: Pearson Prentice Hall, 2004.
Girl Source	*Girl Source: A Book by and for Young Women About Relationships, Rights, Futures, Bodies, Minds, and Souls.* Berkeley, CA: Ten Speed Press, 2003.
Sharon K. Jackson	*Who's Watching Your Drink.* Grand Rapids, MI: Norton, 2004.
Michael S. Kimmel	*The Gender of Desire: Essays on Male Sexuality.* Albany, NY: SUNY Press, 2005.
Elaine Landau	*Date Violence.* New York: Scholastic Library Publishing, 2004.
Teresa M. Lauer	*The Truth About Rape.* Blaine, WA: Lauer Group, 2002.
Kristen J. Leslie	*When Violence Is No Stranger: Pastoral Counseling with Survivors of Acquaintance Rape.* Minneapolis: Augsburg Fortress, 2004.
Barrie Levy	*In Love and in Danger: A Teen's Guide to Breaking Free of Abusive Relationships.* New York: Regan, 2001.
Carrie L. Lukas	*The Politically Incorrect Guide to Women, Sex, and Feminism.* Washington, DC: Regenery Publishing, 2006.

Aphrodite
Matsakis

*The Rape Recovery Handbook: Step-
by-Step Help for Survivors of Sexual
Assault.* Oakland, CA: New Harbinger
Publications, 2003.

Joan McGregor

*Is It Rape?: On Acquaintance Rape
and Taking Women's Consent Seriously.* Aldershot, UK: Ashgate, 2005.

James Newton
Poling and
Christie Cozad
Neuger, eds.

*Men's Work in Preventing Violence
Against Women.* Binghamton, NY:
Haworth Press, 2003.

Jeffrey Scott
Shapiro and
Jennifer Stevens

Kobe Bryant: The Game of His Life.
Portland, OR: Revolution Publishing,
2004.

Michael Smalley,
Amy Smalley, and
Mike Yorkey

Don't Date Naked. Carol Stream, IL:
Tyndale House, 2003.

Jennifer Temkin

Rape and the Legal Process. New York:
Oxford University Press, 2003.

Alan Wertheimer

Consent to Sexual Relations. Cambridge, U.K.: Cambridge University
Press, 2003.

Joan Zorza

Violence Against Women. Kingston,
NJ: Civic Research Institute, 2004.

Periodicals

Antonia Abbey

"Alcohol-Related Sexual Assault: A
Common Problem Among College
Students," *Journal of Studies on Alco-
hol,* March 2002.

American
Association of
Family Physicians

"Sexual Health: Rape and Date
Rape," WebMD.com, February 9,
2007.

Lisa Bennett

"Attacks on Campus Feminism
Spread Misinformation, Propaganda,"
National NOW Times, Summer 2002.

Ray Blumhorst

"VAWA—One of the Biggest Tax-
payer Fleecings in the History of
America," ifeminists.com, March 16,
2005.

Kadence
Buchanan

"Avoid Being the Next Date Rape
Victim," Ezine Articles, August 31,
2006.

CBS News.com

"Army Rape Accuser Speaks Out,"
February 20, 2005.

Sarah Conly

"Seduction, Rape, and Coercion,"
Ethics, October 2004.

Peta Cooper

"Date Rape—Can It Happen to
You?" DesiClub.com, February 2004.

Lauren Fischetti
and Allison
Stevens

"Duke Rape Charges Highlight Common Campus Danger," Women
eNews, April 2, 2006.

Gregory Flannery

"Military Rape: The Ugly Secret in
the American Armed Forces," *Cincin-
nati City Beat*, August 22–28, 2002.

Freelance Star

"Was It Rape? Duke Case Shows
Problem of Prosecuting Sex Crimes,"
May 1, 2006.

Michelle Guido   "State Court Defines Rape Ruling:
                      Women May Withdraw Consent at
                      Any Point," *San Jose Mercury News*,
                      January 6, 2003.

Harvard School   "Prevalence of Rape Higher in Heavy
of Public Health   Drinking College Environments,"
                      February 12, 2004.

Annika Howard   "Juries Reluctant to Convict in Rape
                      Cases in Which Alcohol Involved,"
                      Crime.about.com, December 6, 2006.

Jordana R. Lewis   "Date Rape Happens at Harvard,"
                      Harvard Crimson, November 13,
                      2005.

Dahlia Lithwick   "Rape Nuts: Kobe Bryant's Trial Will
                      Showcase Our Mixed-up Rape Laws,"
                      Slate.com, July 30, 2003.

Theodore W.   "Perceptions of Appropriate Punish-
McDonald   ment for Committing Date Rape:
                      Male College Students Recommend
                      Lenient Punishments," *College Stu-
                      dent Journal*, March 2004.

Wendy McElroy   "When Is It Rape?" ifeminists.net,
                      January 14, 2003.

Miles Moffeit and   "Female GIs Report Rapes in Iraq
Amy Herdy   War," *Denver Post*, January 25, 2004.

Jessica Mousseau   "The Truth About Date Rape: Vic-
                      tims Live in Haunting Anguish," As-
                      sociatedContent.com.

Rachel O'Byrne, Mark Rapley, and Susan Hansen
"You Couldn't Say 'No,' Could You?: Young Men's Understandings of Sexual Refusal," *Feminism & Psychology*, Volume 16, 2006.

Jennifer L. Pozner
"Columnist Dishes Dangerous Logic About Rape," WomensNews.com, April 26, 2006.

Sarah Price
"Date Rape Victims May Be Spiking the Truth," *Sun-Herald* (Sydney, Australia), August 21, 2005.

Naomi Schaefer Riley
"Ladies, You Should Know Better: How Feminism Wages War on Common Sense," *Wall Street Journal*, April 14, 2006.

Trudy W. Schuett
"Betrayal of Women—VAWA 2005," ifeminists.net, June 15, 2005.

Starman
"Myths About Male Rape, the Rape of Men," AEST.org, September 26, 2006.

Courtney Stuart
"How UVA Turns Its Back on Rape," *Hook*, November 11, 2004.

Andrew E. Taslitz
"Willfully Blinded: On Date Rape and Self-Deception," *Harvard Journal of Law and Gender*, Volume 28, 2005.

S. Thompson
"Date Rape in Criminal Law," AssociatedContent.com, October 19, 2006.

Cathy Young
"Yes Means No: Troubling Questions About Rape and Consent," *Boston Globe*, January 20, 2003.

Index

DATE DUE

OCT 1 5 2008		
DEC 0 3 2008		
DEC 1 9 2009		
DEC 1 9 2011		

DEMCO 38-296